a daughter too many

My Journey to Find Family and Forgiveness

KARI E. WISEMAN

W. Brand Publishing

NASHVILLE, TENNESSEE

Some names and places have been changed to protect individuals in the story.

j.brand@wbrandpub.com

W. Brand Publishing

www.wbrandpub.com

Cover design by JuLee Brand / designchik.net

A Daughter To Many/ Kari E. Wiseman. —1st ed.
Available in Paperback, Kindle, and eBook formats.
Paperback ISBN: 978-1-950385-06-5
Hardcover ISBN: 978-1-950385-09-6
eBook ISBN: 978-1-950385-07-2
Library of Congress Control Number: 2019904629

contents

dedication

I dedicate this book to my Forever Father,
out of eternal gratitude for His faithfulness to me.

I also dedicate it to my family, that is, all of the people who have
helped support me and shape me into who I am today.
(There are hundreds in this family!)

Special dedication goes to my mother, my father,
and my brothers. You have loved me in spite of me.

To my husband Drew and our children, my life would be
incomplete without you in it.

May this book bring you healing and hope as it reminds us that:
He is always with those who serve Him,
He loves us way more than we can imagine,
and that He chooses to forgive us when we fail Him.
I love you more than I can share
or show, so this written work of love is for you.

PREFACE

I have had three different first and middle names, four different last names, but I have only been married one time. I have moved 25 times, lived in 11 cities in nine states, and no, my family was not in the military. I have had six sets of grandparents, but I am an only child. Looking back, the one constant thread has been that the Lord's hand has held mine throughout all of my life, regardless of where I was physically, emotionally, or even spiritually. He has proven this by providing countless parental figures and families who would walk through life's moments with me by encouraging, guiding and loving me along the way.

Many hours have been devoted to deciding the best method of telling this story. With so many angles and twists and turns, it certainly gets extremely confusing. What I have discovered is that if I tell this in the order of how I remember these events, then you can follow along better. By the end of this book, you will have experienced the depths of anger and sadness, the peaks of joy and gladness, and the unfathomable mercy and grace of our God, testifying to His *personal* involvement in our lives.

Some of the names of those involved in this story have been changed to protect their identity. Please be aware that this book contains situations that are rather delicate in nature, therefore this is not for younger readers.

I'm adopted!

I have always known that I was adopted. It was obvious too. I did not look like my mom or dad or two brothers. They all had these normal, cute little noses, and I did not. I had these dark, sunken circles under my eyes, but they did not. I was the black sheep of the family too—it was as though nothing I did was right or good enough. Naturally, as I became a little older, I began to wonder what my birth family was like. *Would they have loved me more? Would they have treated me differently? Did I look like them? Did I have a sister or brother? Why was I not living with them?* As a result of these many questions, when I was around ten years old, my mom had some investigating done by an uncle of mine who was an attorney in Rapid City, South Dakota. He uncovered some interesting facts of which my mom and dad were not aware. Between what he discovered and the adoption papers that my parents had, I was able to piece together enough basic information to learn about my history. Perhaps this would give me some insight as to who I really was, and why.

My name was Andrea June, and when I was 21 months old, my family gave me up for adoption. They turned me over to an adoption agency, Lutheran Social Services, in Sioux Falls, South Dakota. I was immediately placed with a loving foster family who had also taken in several other children. I don't remember any details of either family since I was so very young. My only memory of that time was when I was nearly two years old: *I am walking down some steps from upstairs to the main floor of a house. The wall is to my right, so I am looking left, out to the room below me. What I remember most vividly is my shoes—they were those little patent leather-like white shoes that laced up the front with just a couple of eyelets, and I had a little silver bell attached to each shoe. The sound of those little bells rang out as I was walking down the steps. I was heading downstairs to meet a family who was considering adopting me!*

This new family had two young sons already. They desperately wanted a little girl, since the mother couldn't have any more children of her own due to health reasons. Their oldest son was three and a half years old, and their other son was almost one year old. The one-year-old was a paraplegic due to being born with an open spine and had multiple major health problems, ranging from having seizures on a regular basis to needing a shunt in his skull, to being paralyzed from the chest down. He wasn't supposed to live even for one year, but he kept surviving his many surgeries. He had spent most of his young life so far in the hospital.

For this reason, he wasn't able to visit me that day in the foster home. The rest of the family was visiting to see if their older son would like me and to see if I could like them.

The parents had been told that for the first visit, no interaction was allowed, only observing me. Well, as soon as they entered the living room, the older boy immediately broke the rules by approaching me and asking if we could go play in my room. I was to be his sister, and he wanted to play and share his favorite book with me! Surprisingly, no one stopped him. The "play date" went well, because he later asked his mom why everyone kept calling me Andrea. You see, he and his parents had already picked out a new name for whoever was to be his new sister, and from his point of view, I had been chosen.

My health at the time was terrible, partly due to apparent neglect by my previous family. I weighed 20 pounds at 22 months old. I had a heart murmur, vaginal infection, head lice, and a very ashy complexion. My eyes were dark and sunken, my hair was short and straw-like, and I couldn't breathe through my nose, nor did I know how to, because it had been plugged shut for so long with thick mucus. Needless to say, when my potential new mother saw me for the first time, it nearly broke her heart. This was not the picture of her new little girl whom she had envisioned! No long curly hair, no chubby little legs and cheeks, no cute dresses, and definitely not one who would curl up in her lap and snuggle. No, I was a little, crazed creature who appeared more like an orphaned child from a third world country! This mom's heartbreak for me because of my physical condition was quickly overruled by her desire to have a daughter, regardless of what shape I was in. So, fortunately for me, this new family found room in their hearts to take me into their lives and their home.

My mom writes this detailed memory as though it happened yesterday:

"*The social services agency gave us clearance to pick up our new daughter on Wednesday. We were so excited to finally bring her home! The Sunday before, we were celebrating our youngest son's birthday and my parents and brothers were going to spend the day with us. Knowing that they wouldn't be able to make the long trip back to our home for quite a while, I called the foster mother and asked if she and her husband could possibly take Andrea for a little "ride" and then drive slowly by our house where we would all be looking out the picture window so my extended family could get a glimpse of our new daughter. They agreed that would work and they would call before they left home and would hold her up to the passenger side window. The call came in the afternoon that they were on their way. We all pushed up to the living room window and waited. A car came slowly down our street, pulled up to the curb and stopped. We could hardly believe it when they got out of the car and the foster mother, carrying Andrea, came up our walk! We flung the door open, made introductions, and they said to my parents, 'We just couldn't drive by and not let you see and hold your new granddaughter. Nobody will know we came a few days early.' With that, everyone sat and visited. I served birthday cake and coffee, and Andrea just took off on a run that never stopped for the hour visit in her new home—upstairs, downstairs, in and out of every room at record speed. Once in a while, someone would catch her as she passed by, but she would wiggle free and take off again. We also found out that day that she was not only fast, curious and unstoppable, but she was also loud, as she screamed "Wheeeeeeeee" as she ran past. There was no question that she would transition easily from foster family to new family in just three days.*"

By the time I turned two years old in April, just two months after they initially met me, I had moved in with them in Sioux Falls, South Dakota, with two little boxes of my sparse belongings. I was officially adopted a few months later, given a new name of Kari Ellen Larsen, and yes, that's the name my older brother called me the first day we met at the foster home.

As I was researching my history, I found a beautiful note that mom had written in her diary. Reading this made me realize that in spite of the many issues we would face in our lives, from the very beginning, she really loved me. This brief poem speaks volumes of how most adoptive parents feel about their new children.

The Answer to an Adopted Child
"Not flesh of my flesh, nor bone of my bone,
but still miraculously my own.
Never forget for a single minute,
you didn't grow under my heart,
but in it."
–1968

I had been living with the Larsens for about one year when I witnessed how having a handicapped sibling could be a challenge. One day my younger brother was in his playpen while mom was in the kitchen. He was laying on his stomach quietly playing when he somehow pulled himself up the side of his playpen, only to fall backward. When he landed, his legs went *snap*. He didn't cry out in pain though since he was paralyzed and couldn't feel it. But when mom heard that *snap* sound from the kitchen, she immediately knew that he had broken something. She quickly scooped him up, grabbed me and my older brother, and we raced to the ER. Upon check-in, the nurse asked mom what had happened, and she tried to explain to her that he broke his legs in the playpen and that he was paralyzed, but the nurse didn't seem to be buying that story. This was in the day when child abuse was more in the public eye, and if a nurse or doctor suspected any potential abuse, they had to look into it further, even report it. It took some time, but once they received my little brother's hospital records and learned the truth of his handicaps, they did not report her.

As luck would have it, about a week later, mom was back in the kitchen preparing dinner. I walked up to her and told her I wanted to go outside and play. She replied, "When I am done." I didn't like her answer, so I said it again, this time with more passion, "I want to go now." She repeated, "When I am done, I will take you outside." That answer did not please me, so with an unhappy growl, I turned my little three-year-old self around and ran straight toward the door to go outside but didn't realize that although the front door was open, the interior glass door with the screen was closed. I ran directly into that door face first! The shattered pieces sliced up my face. Mom loaded us into her car and drove back to the same ER with blood running down my little face. Explaining to the check-in nurse that her daughter just ran into the glass door caused even more questions since they checked our records and noticed that mom had just brought my brother in a week ago! *What mom can make up such things?* I must have corroborated her story because they didn't report her that time either. This account is just an example of what a strong-willed child I was even at three.

That same year in the fall of '69, we moved several hours east to White Bear Lake, Minnesota, because my dad had gotten a management job at a rental store. We moved into a small two-bedroom apartment, where I learned many things that a child learns at that age, such as how to swim in the pool. I remember my dad would throw coins into the water, encouraging me to jump in and pick them up. Eventually, he had me diving in the deep end. Each time I accomplished it, he let me keep the coins that I picked up. No doubt I didn't earn a lot of money because after all, this was a short Minnesota summer. Mom told me of one afternoon that fall when a neighbor from the apartment beneath us claimed that as she was preparing dinner, she looked out and had seen me squatting to pee outside her ground-level window. Good thing it was only a pee squat! We lived in this apartment complex for about two years.

My parents built a brand-new house that we moved into before I started kindergarten. It was a rambler-style home with a full basement. These days we call it a ranch. It was on a one-third acre lot across the street from our local junior high school. A couple of years after we moved in, my handicapped brother actually moved home from the hospital! He had been living in four different hospitals for the majority of the first seven years of his life, had endured about 20 surgeries, and now he was healthy and strong enough for us to take care of him on our own. Because he was paralyzed from the chest down, had a stoma, a shunt, and a history of seizures, someone had to be near him 24/7. He needed help with every daily task—lifting him from his bed to the wheelchair, getting him on the toilet and back to his wheelchair, bathing, getting dressed, preparing special foods that he could eat, giving him all of his meds and taking care of his colostomy bag. He went to a special school for children with disabilities and got picked up in a specialized van, but often he was too sick or had to be hospitalized for more surgeries. Even though his care was very stressful on us, especially on my parents, we all loved him. He had such a cheerful personality and loved to giggle, so there were a lot of laughs. I called him my six-million-dollar brother because of his costly hospital bills.

Since he needed to be closer to my parents' bedroom, downstairs I went. Dad built a nice bedroom for me, with smoky white and grey paneling. For the twin bed, mom picked out a brass headboard with a scrolled pattern. It was very girlie, and it made me feel quite special! She made a bed cover that was a pretty light blue large-checked fabric, and she used the same fabric to wrap around the vanity. A three-way mirror sat on the vanity that was nearly two feet tall, and three feet wide when opened up. Behind the draped fabric of the vanity were a couple of shelves to store my favorite things. A small brass stool covered in the same fabric sat in front of the vanity. Above my bed was a basement window that was about seven feet off of the ground. The closet had a rod with some cloth across it that I would slide over to get to my clothes. There was a tiny nightstand with a radio and clock next to my bed. I also had my own bathroom which had a small sink, a toilet, and a stand-up shower. Dad would need to use it on occasion when he came home from work since the laundry room was adjacent to my bathroom.

Thinking about the radio beside my bed made me recall one of my favorite nighttime memories. At approximately 9:05 pm on Thursday nights (don't quote me on the exact time and day), a weekly program would come on the radio. I was not allowed to stay up late and have my radio on, but on these particular nights, I just couldn't go to sleep! I would wait for 9:04 pm, turn my radio on with the volume down low and my lights off, hoping my parents wouldn't find out. You see, the "*Radio Mystery Theater*" was playing, with its chilling scary stories of mystery. This child's imagination went wild with those sounds of creaking doors opening slowly, only to reveal . . . ahhhh!! I would find myself so tightly curled up under the covers, hugging my blanket like it was my only safety between me and whatever was behind those doors. I wasn't afraid of the dark—*how could I be with my bedroom in the basement*—but I was afraid of things under my bed and what might jump out from behind those creaky doors. I think even Vincent Price would have been scared listening to these radio stories.

Mom was truly a gifted music teacher and had been one since she was in high school. She taught piano, of which we had three; she taught folk guitar, of which we had several; and she taught organ . . . fortunately we had only one. She would teach piano and organ out of our spare front bedroom we called the Music Room, which was also our library. It was the room adjacent to the front door. She would teach mostly children after school from 3-6 pm. During these lessons, I was on a strict schedule every day, which was written down on legal-sized paper, down to the half hour. This kept me out of trouble, most of the time. I had to practice piano and violin, do homework, watch my little brother, and stay quiet or go outside to play until dad got home. My older brother James was also on a schedule. He had more practice time than I did since he played drums, guitar, bass clarinet, piano, and violin. Our home was always filled with the sounds of music, though it didn't always sound very good or in tune.

Dad worked very hard at the rental store. He would typically work Monday through Friday, sun up to sundown, then come home exhausted and try to take a quick 20-minute nap on the couch to recharge his batteries. This wasn't easy for him to do since my mom was still teaching music lessons and we kids were going stir-crazy. One weekend we couldn't find dad anywhere, making mom very nervous. We hunted everywhere! Eventually, we found him, napping in the tiny foyer closet. We only discovered him because his hand had fallen out of the slightly open door, causing mom to have a near heart attack since she believed he had died! He had just been trying to find a quiet place to nap. Let me tell you he had to have been extremely desperate to go in there, since he was sitting on the floor, leaning against the side wall amidst all the year-round garb of four people—the shoes, winter boots, scarves, mittens and gloves, snowmobile suits and about 20 coats and jackets.

Now my dad was a true Jack-of-all-trades, a handyman, which I think rubbed off on me. I loved following him around and attempting to help as he would paint the house, or dig post holes for putting up a fence, or create walls for the rooms in the basement that became our kitchen and my bedroom, or do any carpentry work with his many saws, drills, tools, etc., in the garage. He could do plumbing, electrical, carpentry, or repair anything. I was like his shadow whenever I could be. My favorite smell was that of sawdust after he would cut wood. To this day, I would much rather be working in the yard, digging in the dirt, mowing, designing and building a cat house or dog house, painting the walls, or trimming branches, than cleaning my house. This passion for hard work reflects well on my dad.

Our parents spent a lot of quality time with us, in spite of their busy schedules and having a handicapped child. They liked playing many yard games with us such as playing ball, badminton, and Frisbee. They took our family camping in the summer nearly every weekend, and they played ping pong with us in our basement, along with card games and board games. We'd play Life, Probe, Chutes and Ladders, Pit, Canasta, Hearts, Rummy, War, and Old Maid to name a few. We were a game-playing family. In fact, we tried to make every Friday night a family game night! I guess that is why today I absolutely love—well, to be more specific, I am truly passionate—about playing games.

Our summers were a blast. We had a pontoon boat that we would take to our cabin. We would fish off the sides, get pulled around in the water on a tube, and just hang out together with our extended family. We also had a tiny wooden camper we called the "chicken coop" that we would take around to local campgrounds and stay. We'd go canoeing, all five of us. Now, this was extremely difficult since my little brother was limited to sitting in his wheelchair. My dad got around this by putting two canoes side by side, strapping two strong poles parallel to each other onto each canoe, creating a base for my little brother's chair to sit on in between the two canoes. My little brother just loved being there with us and being taller than we were! When we would go hiking, my dad would put him on this large backpack with a metal frame and padded base and strap it to his back so he could carry my brother around with us. No doubt as he grew, so did the weight on dad. Eventually, my parents bought a better camper, a Jayco pop-up type that slept six people. This was a much better sleeping arrangement for the five of us when we'd go camping.

There were many other fun family memories that I fondly recall. For example, at Halloween, usually rather than trick-or-treating, we'd be playing Bingo and winning candy for ourselves, winning coins for our Unicef boxes, and passing out candy to the trick-or-treaters who came to our door. For me, this was more fun than going out and getting candy. Our ping pong tournaments, held in the basement, were great fun, but sometimes a little more challenging when we would push my little brother's wheelchair up to the table and have him playing with us. My parents always tried to include him in our family activities. If we were playing baseball in the back yard, often that meant pushing him in his chair from home base all the way around the bases and back home to give him a winning score. He thrived on the attention, and it made us all happy to see him smile.

My early childhood years were pretty typical, as far as "normal" goes. But as I got closer to becoming a "tween," events in my life started taking a downward turn. Therefore, I feel the need to point out to you that from this time forward, the reading is for more mature people. Please keep in mind that these instances from my childhood are all written from my perspective as a child, my memories of being a child, but know that it is all true. There are many sides to any story, but only one truth. I have forgiven my parents because God has forgiven me. None of us are perfect! Nonetheless, the following verse sums up what Satan was able to accomplish, but know that God is ever present and allowed it all to be for a reason: "... *you meant evil against me, but God meant it for good in order to bring about this present result, to preserve many people alive.*" (Genesis 50:20 NAS)

trouble

My parents were firm believers in punishment. Dad would usually be the one to spank us, sometimes with his hand, a belt, or a board. I got in trouble much more than my older brother did, but he wasn't spared punishment. Mine just seemed more severe and was often more unusual.

For instance, one winter evening when I was about 11 and after dad dropped me off for choir practice at church, a girl-friend and I decided it would be great fun to hide during practice in the choir robes area, which was like a very large closet located in the back of the choir room. We were so well disguised that no one saw us or heard us, even though we giggled throughout most of it. When the hour-long practice was over, we snuck out of the room and went outside to get picked up by our parents. What I didn't know was that the choir teacher had seen me get dropped off but didn't see me during practice. She was so concerned about it that she called my house immediately following practice and was very surprised to hear my dad say that I had been there and had been picked up as usual. My parents had *busted* me! So, to catch me in the lie, they called me upstairs (remember my bedroom was in the basement) and asked how choir practice was. Naturally, I replied, "Fine." In my mind, there was no way of them knowing the truth. That was when they lowered the boom and told me that my teacher had called them out of concern for me not being there. *Ohhh no.*

I kept trying to lie about it and say that I was there but eventually had to confess that I was hiding in the robes closet the entire time. Well, lying led to punishment in my house. Honestly, I lied quite a bit. I lied so much, that when I would actually tell the truth, I didn't know how to act. My web of lies was beginning to entangle me. So, this time my dad sent me out into the cold garage, but first had me remove all of my clothes except for my underwear and told me that I was going to get a spanking. I went out and waited a few minutes for my dad to come out. As I waited for him, I was shaking–from the Minnesota cold, from fear of being punished, and from fear of this new unknown method. After a few minutes of mental torture, dad came out. He removed his belt, but then also removed his t-shirt. Wow, did he have white skin! It was in the middle of winter in Minnesota, probably about 10 degrees outside, therefore very, very cold in our garage. As I stood there, quite uncomfortable and bewildered, he told me that my punishment was actually to whip *him* with the belt across his back rather than me getting whipped. He explained that Jesus took our punishment by being beaten and whipped so that we might be saved. Dad wanted me to feel the pain of causing him pain, and that would help me not want to lie again. It was supposed to hurt me to hurt him! He insisted that I had to hit him ten good times across his back, and that if I didn't make it hurt, then I had to do it again until it was right. I slowly picked up his leather belt and began. Tears were streaming down my face for causing him so much pain, but I hit him over and over, many times being told it wasn't hard enough. By the time I was done, his entire back was red with deep welts, totaling about forty of them. (Ironic–it was thought that Jesus received thirty-nine lashes before his crucifixion because if it had been forty, the criminal was said to have died.) After I had given him sufficient hits, I was only then allowed to get dressed and go back inside the house to go to bed. My pillow was soaked that night from tears. By the way, this unusual punishment was not my dad's original idea. I recently discovered it came from a religious tract which is fortunately no longer available. *I wonder why*? I can tell you that even though I understood even what they were trying to teach, it is *not* the best method of punishment.

Dinner was often another unhappy time for me. Typically, I devoured my food and even ate everyone else's scraps, but occasionally I did not like what was being served, so I would either eat very slowly, hoping when everyone else was done that I could be too, or I would just refuse to eat it at all. Yes, I was a very stubborn little girl! Now there were consequences for this. If I was the last one eating and was going too slowly, then I might have to stand up to finish my meal. If that didn't get the job done in a timely manner, then I was to stand on one leg.

I remember one night I just didn't like what we were having, so there I was, standing at the table. Now we enjoyed watching evening game shows like Match Game or some other family show in the kitchen. This particular evening the little neighbor boy was coming over to watch television with my younger brother after dinner. I was standing there, not eating, embarrassed, and I really, really had to go to the bathroom. Not to get rid of the nasty food, but I honestly did have to go! My parents decided I had to wait until I was all done eating. It was a standoff, literally. I lasted as long as I could, but in a way, they won because I wound up peeing on the floor and had to stand in this puddle of pee while the neighbor boy was sitting just a few feet from me. He never came back over after that. *I wonder why?*

Perhaps, since I was so scrawny as a young girl, that would explain why I hoarded my food—at least the food I liked. Mom would tell me at dinnertime I would take way more food than I could possibly eat, and then scarf it down before anyone else had even finished serving themselves. I also would steal food whenever possible. Since we had that kitchen downstairs with canned goods and frozen things, I had ample opportunity to take what I wanted but had to find a way to dispose of the evidence before mom could find it. Yes, I was somewhat devious. There was one time that I took a can of tuna, opened it up, and began eating it quickly, right out of the can. That tuna smell started permeating everywhere, and I panicked. I chowed down as much as I could, which wasn't a lot because it gets pretty thick and dry. I then hid the can in my bedroom vanity, not knowing what else to do with it.

Later when mom came down to check on me, she obviously smelled it but couldn't find it. I told her I didn't know why my room smelled like tuna, and no, I didn't have any. That partially eaten can of tuna sat in my vanity for several days, stinking more and more, until I couldn't take it any longer. I peeked under the vanity curtain, took the can out, and realized it had begun molding. *Phew*! I threw it out in the garbage upstairs while mom was teaching a piano lesson, hoping desperately that no one would find it. Of course, mom did.

Now don't let me paint a picture of these horrible parents and this poor misunderstood child. My parents had a lot to deal with, especially having a handicapped child with special needs. Nor was I an angel. In fact, I could be quite the handful and mischievous! In our house around Christmas time, my parents would put our presents from them under the Christmas tree early, sometimes three to four weeks early. The sticky part was that the tree was in the basement, and so was my room. That meant that I would have to walk past those gifts multiple times a day, sometimes for weeks. Naturally being a curious kid with no adults around, I decided to sneak a peek. All I had to do was gently unstick the tape from the end, and the rest was easy. Well, when I was twelve, I did just that with *all* of my presents under the tree. In years past, I had only managed one or two.

Not this time! I was so excited to see what they were giving me!

After dinner that same evening, Mom and Dad called me upstairs to the main kitchen and told me to bring all of my presents with me. Strange. Nervously, I obeyed. Mom then admitted that from the top of the stairs they had witnessed me opening my gifts and that I had to take them all to my room, open them up and enjoy them *now*. It was still two weeks before Christmas! Needless to say, I was very saddened by this and felt terrible, but was happy to open them again. The bummer was that on Christmas Eve when everyone opened up the family gifts one at a time, I had nothing of mine to open. I had to wait until Christmas morning to get my presents from

Santa. Those were in our stocking, so not much excitement there. Usually, it consisted of a Book of Life Savers candy and a couple of other small things. As a result, I never opened up my presents early again.

My mom and I struggled with our relationship from early on. She couldn't understand why I wasn't more loving and girlie, and I couldn't understand how to make her happy. As a mother and daughter, we always seemed to clash—not physically, but emotionally. There was one thing we did that made each of us happy: I discovered that she loved to have her hair combed. Knowing this, sometimes in the evenings after dinner, I would get her comb, have her sit in a kitchen chair, and I played with her hair. I would comb it, part it, put barrettes in it, and then mess it all up and do it all over again. When I messed it all up, it was called the 'blow dryer.' She would practically fall asleep every time! It relaxed her, which pleased me. This was our bonding time, though it didn't last more than thirty minutes. Soon I was back in trouble for misbehaving or lying. I remember one evening I had done something wrong which made her mad, so when I tried to give her a kiss goodnight, she turned her head and said, "I don't want a Judas kiss." Growing up in the church, I knew exactly what that meant. (Judas, one of Jesus' twelve disciples, betrayed him in the garden by giving Jesus a kiss; this showed the soldiers which man was to be arrested. Jesus was consequently arrested and put on trial which led to his death.)

Across the street from our house was the back of the junior high school. I loved going over there and running on the track, skating on the three hockey rinks, playing tennis and riding my bike around. One evening while mom was preparing dinner, rather than help her as she had asked, I chose to go riding my bike for a bit by the hockey rinks until it was time to eat. Soon the sky started to darken. I watched for several minutes as the blackest clouds I had ever seen came rolling in. The dark skies scared me a bit, so I decided it was time for me to get home. I looked toward the house which was several hundred feet away across the track and soccer field. All of a sudden, I saw the garage door open and our van back out, turn right and drive away down the street. *Who was leaving?* I pedaled as fast as I could for home to see if it was time to eat and to escape the approaching storm. With the wind blowing much harder and the rain beginning to fall, I quickly ran to the side door and tried to open it. It was locked! They never locked the door except at night and when we were gone. *Had they all left?* I went to the main front door, and it too was locked. I ran around to the back door, getting quite scared, and it was locked as well. I considered breaking a window to get in, but that would mean serious trouble for me later. *Now, what do I do? Where do I go?* All I could think of was riding my bike the mile to my friend Stephanie's house. She lived by our elementary school. By now the storm was fully upon me as the rain came down hard and the strong winds tried to blow me over on my bike. I pedaled as fast as I could, crying the whole way. *Why had they left me? Did they forget about me? Was I going to survive this? Did they leave on purpose to teach me a lesson?*

I made it to my friend's house in about seven minutes. I knocked on the front door, and Stephanie opened it. I stood there, soaking wet, cold, and scared. She immediately said she couldn't play because they had company over. *Play?* I just wanted to find a safe, dry place! Her parents let me in and dried me off the best they could. Their questions about why in the world was I out in this and not home gave me the chance to tell them my sob story. The storm blew over a large tree that was in their front yard moments after I arrived. It was a terrible storm. I was exhausted, cold, wet and emotionally devastated. My family had left me. They had left me out in the storm. After trying to call them for two hours, dad finally answered the home phone, and I told him where I was. When he picked me up, I asked him why they left me. Apparently, my parents were upset with me for not helping prepare dinner. They decided to have dinner out, so they left. Little did they know just how much their punishment affected me.

Every little girl dreads her first period. Mine came when I was ten. It was bedtime around 9:00 pm, so I was downstairs in my room when I felt this strange sensation. I went into the bathroom, only to discover blood. I didn't know much about periods, so I ran upstairs to my parents' room and told them that I thought I had started my period. They had the television on while getting ready for bed. Mom was already lying down and showed no sign of getting up to help me. *Did she even hear me?* It was dad who went into their bathroom, grabbed mom's box of OB tampons, and walked me downstairs to my bathroom. Yep, he showed me how to use one. I was absolutely horrified that he did this, but someone had to show me what to do! *Is this incident what led to his future actions and my heartache?*

During that same year, dad began acting strangely toward me. I recall one evening as I was reading a book in my bed that he came into my room and asked me if I was OK. *Yep, I was fine.* He proceeded to tell me that he had to check and see if I was healthy and growing right by looking at my private area. *What? No, this isn't right.* This isn't how it's done or who checks me out. I tried to argue and tell him I was fine, and that he shouldn't be doing this. He was my dad though, and maybe he did have to since I hadn't been to the doctor in a while. It didn't feel right though. This led to other visits in my room that involved touching my breasts and wanting me to touch him. Dad explained to me that mom was sick and couldn't do certain things with or for him.

Since my bedroom was in the basement of our home, he had easy access to me. He would just come home from work, get cleaned up in the laundry room, then try to sneak a peek, or ask me for a favor, or just need to touch me. One time he even showed me his large stash of Penthouse magazines that he had hidden in the garage. According to him, I needed to see what sex looked like. He thought I needed to learn how to perform these acts by my practicing with a hotdog. *It took a couple of decades for me to eat those again.* He tried to have intercourse with me in the small main bathroom one time, and I told him he was too big for me, but he kept on trying. He attempted this on many occasions. When he would come home from work, I remember hiding from him so that he wouldn't try something.

How do you tell someone about that? Mom wasn't exactly going to believe me since I had been lying to her so much lately. *Why did he have to come into my room when the lights were out and try to have sex with me? Why when he was trying to nap on the basement couch after work and mom was teaching music would he try to pull me close to lay with him so he could touch me?* I was learning a perverted view of sex.

This went on for nearly three years. The few people that I did tell didn't believe me. No one would believe that a church-going family with a handicapped child and an adopted child would have this kind of problem. We were viewed as good people. We attended church every Sunday morning, many Sunday evenings, Wednesday evenings, and were in Sunday school and choir. *No, it just wasn't possible.*

When I was eleven, my parents decided that I was out of control and needed some professional help. They had already sent me to my grandparents' and my aunts' and uncles' homes during the summers, but I was still acting out. Perhaps it was my choice of friends or the skimpy clothes that I would sneak to school under my proper clothes, or my constant lying, but something much more drastic had to happen, someone else had to intervene. They set up a meeting for me with a counselor through the Lutheran Social Services. I remember our first counseling session was on Halloween evening. This counselor tried to convince my parents that I needed to attend their camp program that rehabilitates kids. They do this by requiring you to watch these movies that show perversions and other destructive acts that are supposed to make you *not* want to do them.

It's like brainwashing. You see such terrible things over and over, and you get disgusted by it and therefore never want to do it. Horrible theory, especially for a child. Fortunately, my parents saw the error in their thinking, and I never visited that counselor or agency again.

Little did they know the real reason that I was acting out. Well, at least mom didn't know, and dad couldn't do the math. I knew—it was due to the molestation . . .

CHAPTER 3

Peniel

At twelve years old, my lies were no longer little or white, and petty thievery had begun. Also, I was very close to getting kicked out of school. My intentions to be good were there, but when it suited me and my backside to lie, I didn't hesitate. The numerous methods of punishment—spankings with a board or belt, being grounded, standing in a corner for an hour, standing on one leg at the dinner table and not being allowed to go to the bathroom, resulting in a puddle on the floor, being made to eat my own throw-up if I didn't like what I was eating, having my room messed up, having my radio thrown against the wall, or even being forced to spank my own dad with a belt—didn't seem to help me get any better. Convinced that I was possibly on drugs, my parents searched for some other way to help me. *Was I doing anything worse than the typical twelve year old?* By today's standards, probably not. The multiple threats of a sandwich sign with "FREE" written on both sides being placed on me while standing on the street corner and waiting for someone else to adopt me, also didn't appear to faze me too badly. Inside, however, the threats cut deeply, making me feel even more unwanted. Having exhausted many of my relatives' good natures by letting me spend summers with them, but with no apparent change in my behavior, and having visited a counselor who brought about no results in positive change, my parents decided even more drastic measures had to be taken.

It was on a bitterly cold, February morning that I found myself sitting in a church service in White Bear Lake, Minnesota. Not that this was anything unusual for my family. No, the odd thing was that this wasn't our church we were in. My mom, being a classical guitar teacher, as well as an accomplished piano and organ teacher, had been giving lessons to the pastor of this church. Naturally, being desperate for new suggestions to try and save her daughter from the current destructive path, mom had opened up to the pastor about me and begged for some help and advice. He told her of this school in Wisconsin that a Lutheran pastor and his wife had started a few years ago. Their sole purpose was to help young people who were in trouble to make a change for themselves and their families. They wanted to give kids ranging in age from eight to seventeen years old the chance to turn their lives around and make something of it, by learning about what God had done for them with His son Jesus, and by hopefully accepting Him into their lives. Ohh! Now, this intrigued my mother. She learned that they were going to be speaking and singing at this very church with many of the students soon! Well, that could be the ticket. So, when that day arrived, she gathered the family and away we went to the most unusual church service I had ever been to.

We arrived just in time for the students' singing to begin. Apparently, the entire service was to be led by this school and the pastor. I noticed how many cute boys there were! All of the students had on navy uniforms with white cotton shirts. The boys had ties, the girls wore skirts. They didn't look especially happy to be standing up there though, singing gospel songs and hymns. Then this fourteen year-old boy shared his testimony of how Peniel had changed his life. He didn't have much of a home life before, so he got involved with the wrong crowd, did drugs, drank, and smoked. After his parents sent him to Peniel, he began to see that things could change and he became less angry. Eventually, he decided to accept Jesus into his life, and though he still struggled, at least he was going in the right direction. *Wow! What is this Peniel,* I wondered. *What a funny name, too.* The kids' pastor, Ken Sortedahl, then spoke on what it was all about and how they received their finances. If anyone was interested in furthering and helping support this ministry, donations of any kind would be accepted. *What a cool school,* I thought. Pastor Ken then mentioned that they were located on a farm, and that's when my ears perked up. He described the setting as seventy-seven acres of rolling hills in Wisconsin, an old farmhouse for the living quarters for the boys, trailer homes for the staff and girls, and their own school that taught the A.C.E. curriculum, which is a self-pacing method. They would travel around the country, out east and west, visiting many churches, with several kids giving their testimonies of how Peniel had given them another chance in life. Being only twelve, this sounded like a pretty great place to me.

Early one morning three months later, shortly after I turned thirteen, and with only two weeks left of seventh grade, Mom and Dad told me to pack up a few of my clothes. Now when I say a few, they literally meant just a few, as in three pair of pants, five shirts, and of course my underwear and socks. When I asked them why, they told me I was going to stay at Peniel for a while. A shock ran through my body as if I had just been electrocuted! *Were they really going to go through with this*? "Maybe it will help me," they said. I wasn't exactly sure what my problem was except for lying and not getting along with my mother. *But going away?* They were actually going to send me away, and I knew in my heart that this was serious. In junior high we heard of girls being sent away for getting pregnant, but not for lying. I didn't understand. *How can parents do that? What was so wrong with me that they didn't want me?* Since my brothers were already in school, I didn't even get to say goodbye to them.

We arrived about an hour later at Peniel Christian School. It was a peaceful setting in the hills of Wisconsin with dogs and cats running around, horses out in the field, a few chickens scurrying about, and no kids in sight. *Where were they?* It was about 9:00 am, and apparently, all of the kids were in school. The pastor and his wife greeted us, took my bag, and with a hug goodbye, away went my family. To this point, I had been a little excited about this new venture on a farm, yet also angry with my parents. I now suddenly felt terrified and very alone. My family was gone. Pastor Ken's wife, Melodee, took over and gently led me into one of the trailer homes where the girls were living. They had converted the entire trailer home into bedrooms for about sixteen girls and a couple of counselors. The front room, where I was to stay for the first few weeks, had three sets of bunk beds in it, with wooden drawers on wheels under each bunk, one for each girl's belongings. So, that is why I only brought a few clothes. Space was limited. Other rooms had similar bunk beds and one little bathroom that we all shared. The kitchen had been converted into a bedroom for the two counselors who lived with the girls. The trailer appeared a little run down but was kept pretty neat and clean considering how many people lived in it.

Mrs. Melodee was a no-nonsense kind of woman but she had a warm smile. She gave me a quick rundown of the rules, and then allowed me to go outside and explore the grounds for about an hour until the other children had their break. *Just what kind of place is this?* I still wasn't sure what it was all about or what was supposed to happen with me, but soon enough it would start to make sense. Little did I know that I was to be here for a long, long time. Perhaps if I knew then what Peniel meant . . . *"And Jacob called the name of the place Peniel: for I have seen God face to face, and my life is preserved."* (Genesis 32:30 KJV)

That was Pastor Ken's vision for the children: For them to see God and who He is, realize their need for Him, and start a new life.

There was a brand-new house on the property that was being built in phases. It was a three-bedroom, one-story house with a basement, totaling about 2,000 square feet. The completed basement was currently being used as their private school. Each student had his or her own wooden desk, which really were just cubicles next to each other separated by partitions. It was very quiet down there. In the center of the room was a tall island of sorts, where the kids would stand and grade their own work. The teachers would go around the room, helping anyone who was struggling and keep a sharp eye out for any cheating at the island. Every now and then you would hear someone trying to quote their memorized Bible scripture that was required for the month. This would earn them an outing away from school on Friday afternoons.

These outings were like winning a prize. If you memorized those selected verses by the first Thursday of the month, you were allowed to get out of school at noon that Friday, and go on the planned field trip and each field trip the following weeks of that month, provided your grades were good. The first Friday's trip was usually the best one since most kids didn't do their scripture memory right away. The outings ranged from downhill skiing, to driving to the Twin Cities to attend the Minnesota State Fair, to much cheaper events later in the month such as going hiking, caving near our school or swimming at the lake. The point was to earn your way out of school early for some fun by learning the Word. I was one of those kids who made the outings every week.

It was during the morning break my first day there that I was introduced to the other students. They were all dressed in navy blue uniforms, had on their white shirts and white socks, and most of them wore tennis shoes. No problem deciding what to wear to school anymore! Not that I liked these police-style uniforms, but it did make it easier. It was when I learned of the uniform swimsuits for the girls that I became rather unhappy. They were *not* attractive! Perhaps it was the suit's skirt that hung below your behind that bothered me the most (today those are quite in style...how ironic). Anyway, I met the other students, got acclimated to my surroundings, and just hung out for the next two weeks since school was about to be out for the summer and it was so late in the school year. Yay, I wouldn't start in the classroom until the fall! This did not bother me one little bit, though I wondered why my parents chose to send me there just before school was out.

My third day there, while the other students were in school and the counselors were helping them, I was unattended and again allowed to explore the property some more. I was fascinated by this big, old gnarly tree that was in the boys' front yard. It sat on the hill, overlooking the surrounding countryside. So, I climbed high up into the big branches and looked around at the farmlands. As I sat there on a limb, I noticed a rope dangling from one of the other branches. It got me thinking about my current situation. I had heard of people hanging themselves when they were deeply depressed, and I was most definitely depressed. I had been abandoned, dropped off at a home for troubled kids, and was unsure how long I'd be there, possibly an entire year. I had been abused by my father for several years. I felt ugly, both inside and out. I didn't have many friends back home, and none at this new place. Seeing this rope gave me the perfect solution. It was time to end my life. Nobody would care. *Why would they?* I was a liar, I didn't behave like a good girl, I made my parents miserable, and no one seemed to believe me or want me. So I reached for that frayed rope, held it for a few minutes as I wondered how to tie the hangman's noose, but was overcome with waves of emotion. I couldn't do it. I just couldn't do it! That would be the end, and I would probably go to Hell for committing suicide. I sat there, shaking, realizing that I had almost killed myself, and somehow, slowly, I climbed down. I didn't tell anyone.

Being thirteen years old and arriving as the new kid at a school of about forty children, I had a lot to learn. Many of the kids there had come from broken homes, yet others came from gangs in Brooklyn, New York and Chicago, where drugs, sex, drinking, smoking, rock and roll, swearing and violence were an everyday occurrence. It was quite a variety of kids. I wasn't familiar with most of these things but had to learn about it and pretend I knew about it to "fit in." Not easy to do for someone as naive as I was at the time. Of the forty students there, I'd say ten had seriously heavy, rebellious backgrounds, and the rest of us were just heading down the wrong path in life, dabbling in those things which could eventually hurt us. Before Peniel, we all would use curse words or listen to rock music, or some of the guys wore an earring and had long hair, but all of that needed to change to become the people that Pastor Ken believed we could be.

The school's rules and guidelines were strict and enforced. No smoking or alcohol, no earrings or long hair for the boys, no make-up for the girls until age sixteen, no radios (except when traveling in the vans and even then it was the pastor's or the counselor's choice of positive music), no television, no movies (unless it was a G movie rented by the staff), pants could not be too tight, no shorts for the girls except in gym class, and then it was culottes only, no phone calls from anyone except immediate family until after the first three months and then only with permission, and mail had to be screened before you could open it. Chores had to be done before any free time, and there was a required exercise each weekday morning, which usually consisted of jogging two or three miles. If you so desired, there were longer routes available with Pastor Ken when he wanted to do so. There was a six-inch rule between the boys and girls, meaning **no physical contact** in any way. Bummer! This was designed to help keep those hormones in check, but it was often abused whenever the opportunity arose, and no eyes were watching that could get you in trouble.

I soon had a boyfriend who became my first true love. He was a student from Buffalo, New York, who came to the school about two months after I did. His mother couldn't handle him anymore. He was a pothead, swore, had long hair, and hung out with the wrong crowd. His father had passed away when he was eight, and his mother didn't have the time to raise him, have a job and keep him out of trouble. So, she sent him to Peniel. Now this boy, David, was good looking! He had black-ish hair, brilliant blue eyes, striking features and was in great physical shape. Not bad for a fifteen year old! He liked me too, so we started "going out," and were together most of my five years at Peniel. Since he had lots of experience with girls, and I had never even gotten to first base, I soon learned the joys of breaking the six-inch rule with him. I remember sneaking out at night, along with some of the other couples, and meeting in one of the horse fields just to be together. We got caught a few times, but it didn't stop us. We were in love! I never allowed myself to give in completely though because I just knew the moment I did, that God would allow me to get pregnant as a punishment. We were together for four years straight, and we, along with everyone else, thought we'd get married someday. He had become my best friend too, rather quickly.

Both of us learned from Pastor Ken about what Jesus had done for us. I know David accepted Him into his heart short-ly after I did, though I don't recall the details. I do remem-ber when I did though! Pastor Ken had taken several of the students to a Christian concert in the Twin Cities, a Dallas Holmes and Praise concert. Now I was thirteen, had been raised in a Lutheran home and knew about Jesus, but had never accepted Him or truly understood that He loved me personally in spite of my failures. I had the head knowledge but not the heart knowledge. It was during the invitation at the concert that I prayed to accept Jesus into my heart, to change my ways and to try and walk in His footsteps. Slowly I learned how to grow in my relationship with Jesus. No, I wasn't perfect and struggled daily in being better and making better decisions. I soon discovered a Bible verse that I quickly claimed for many years. It read, *"When my father and my mother forsake me, then the Lord will take me up."* (Psalms 27:10 KJV)

That doesn't mean I wasn't still a little troublemaker though. It was about one month later in the cooler part of October that an older girlfriend and I decided on a whim to run away from the school. There wasn't a good reason to do so, but it just sounded like fun. There had been other kids who ran away because they hated Peniel, but we didn't hate it. We just wanted to run away from there.

It was about 9:00 pm, and nearly dark. The girls were taking turns showering at the big boys' house, the old farmhouse, since our water heater was not working. Penny and I had finished our showers and were heading back to our house when the urge to run away just overcame us. We hardly even discussed it but decided to do it. *Why not?* Never in my life had I done such a crazy and risky thing! We got back to the house, grabbed a few things, and without anyone noticing, snuck out the front door and ran down through the empty cornfield, making our way to the county road. We had gone about two miles when we saw headlights coming in our direction. We hid in the ditch, hoping they wouldn't see us, especially if it was someone from our school. We learned later that it was. We got up and went a few more miles until we took the road that led us to the highway, where we would hitchhike our way to freedom in California! Boy, we were dreaming big for being so small and ignorant. My friend Penny had more worldly experience than I did, and since she was older, she was the leader. It was a foggy, cool night, and by the time we made it to the highway, we were pretty damp. We had gone about eight miles in a couple of hours and were really exhausted. We decided to try and flag down a passing car to get a ride to the nearest big city, Minneapolis. The plan would just have to evolve from there. As luck would have it, a car did slow down and two men about thirty years old offered us a ride to the next small town. Keep in mind that it was around 11 pm, foggy, and we were young, about to hop into a car with two grown men!

We got in. They drove to the next town and found an open liquor store. They parked out front, went inside and bought two six-packs of a cheap beer, Hamm's. Now I did not like beer. My dad drank this beer, and it was terrible. My girlfriend liked it though, so she took them up on their offer and took a can. They seemed nice enough (don't most people with bad intentions?), so we agreed to ride further with them to the Twin Cities. I was getting thirsty, so I reluctantly took a can for myself. (Hint: if you're thirsty, do not drink beer or any other alcohol. I learned the hard way.) Within fifteen minutes, I had to go to the bathroom. That stuff goes right through you! Well, there wasn't any stopping until we got to the city.

We made it to Minneapolis in about forty-five minutes. They drove to a large apartment complex, parked their car, and we all got out. Now it's nearly midnight, and I am starting to get nervous, questioning what their motives were. They casually invited us up to their place, which they stated was on the second floor. My worldly-wise partner in crime naturally accepted for both of us. *What?* We didn't know these guys very well, actually not at all, especially not enough to go into their apartment! I tried quietly to convince her otherwise, but it was cold, late and I just had to go to the bathroom!

Reluctantly I agreed, against my better judgment (hah, not good judgment at all), so we went up into their place. Now, these two guys were pretty drunk by this time, but not too drunk to devise a plan to try to have their way with us. *Had they done this before?* Once inside, one guy led my friend into one of the other rooms, while the other man asked me to sit on his lap in the kitchen on a barstool. *Oh no.* I had to come up with something quickly! I saw a deck of cards sitting there on the counter and asked him if he wanted to play a game. He didn't want to, so I "accidentally" dropped them on the floor anyway so that I would have to pick them up rather than get too close to him. *Man, did I have to go to the bathroom!* I was worried about my friend though. I got up, barely escaping the man's clutches, and went into the room where she was, sitting on the edge of the bed talking to her man. Just then, "my" man decided it was time to be more intimate, so he tried to tackle me to the floor. Penny came to my rescue, trying to make light of it and playing it off as though we were just wrestling and having fun. The other guy came over and wanted to join in. *Oh my.* I needed to go to the bathroom so badly, so I asked my friend to go with me. She quickly agreed, and we went into the bathroom and locked the door. I finally was able to go! *What a relief.* We were trying to organize a plan to get out of there when they came knocking at the door. We said we'd be right out, and could they wait for us in the living room? After deciding to just bust out of there, we threw open the bathroom door, ran for the front door, and tried to get it open. It was locked! Panic quickly set in, so we pulled as hard as we could at the front door with my friend breaking the framing, allowing us to get out just as they were lunging for us. Run! Run! We laughed as we made our escape from those two drunken men, thankful to be intact, and headed for the parking lot.

Once we were safely a good distance away, I realized that I had to go to the bathroom *again.* That darn beer! I had less than one can too. Not seeing anywhere private to go, nor anyone else around, I squatted right there in the middle of a parking lot at about 12:30 am. As my luck would have it, I missed, peeing all over my yellow painter pants. *That's just great.* Now I'm going to smell wonderful as the wee morning hours come around.

The area we were in could be described as a low-rent housing district. I was quite nervous walking around at this hour, in this place, not knowing what was to become of us. We were walking down the sidewalk when I noticed a police car heading our way. We ran a different direction, hoping he didn't see us. A couple of blocks later, a van with three very cute 18-year-olds in it drove up to us. Penny warmed up to them right away, but that police car turned the corner and came our way again. The van quickly drove away, as we ran in another direction. A block later, we met up with the same van.

The guys invited us to join them as they drove around town, listening to the Bee Gees, egging people, smoking pot, and drinking beer.

I refused the beer since I had already had a mishap and drank 7-Up instead. I had never tried marijuana, so opted "no" for that too. We drove around with them for about five hours. I sat pretty much alone due to my aroma of de toilette, and Penny hung with the boys. Did I mention they stole a stereo system from a Burger King? As the sun was about to rise, they headed back to their place. It was an apartment in the upstairs of a house which had been subdivided. Upon arrival, we had woken up their mother. Now I'm not sure which of the boys actually lived here and whose mother it was, but she treated them all like her own and was extremely mad. What had they been doing all night and who were these girls, what was that smell, why did they wake her and so on. We stayed there only long enough for the guys to decide it was time for my friend and me to go. It wasn't until then that they really started to question who we were, why were we running away, where were we going and how were we going to get there? Believe it or not, as two of them drove us to the entrance ramp of the highway where they dropped us off, they scolded us for running away and not facing our problems. It couldn't be that bad they said. Why don't we just call them and go back? Well, because we simply didn't want to, and we had gone too far for that. We said our goodbyes, and off we went, with some fun memories and bizarre stories to tell, and with high hopes of reaching California in a few days.

Walking the interstate on a Sunday morning around 9:00 am isn't exactly the smartest thing to do, especially when you're thirteen and fifteen years old. Obviously, we stuck out like a sore thumb. It wasn't even twenty minutes before a cop pulled over and asked us to get inside his car. Who were we? Where did we live? Why were we out here hitchhiking? Where were our mothers? You would think that two girls who were on the run would talk about these things in advance, maybe even coordinate names, addresses, stories, birthdays, etc. But no, we hadn't finished that yet. We had just begun concocting our version when he pulled over. He wouldn't let us talk on the way to the station, so getting our story straight wasn't in the cards.

We arrived at the police station in Minneapolis, where we were immediately split up. One cop took my friend, and I was sent to the Captain's office. Again, I was asked who I was, where was I going, where did I live and so on. My replies were: a false name, she was my sister, I don't remember our address because we just moved here, our mother was at work but I didn't know the name of her work because she just started there. My birthday, I got right since I used mine. I told him I didn't have a middle name. I said my sister didn't have one either. So far, our little story was working, but the Captain believed that I was someone else who was on the run, so he pushed me a little more for additional information. I had no idea whom he thought I might be, so it wasn't hard to deny any questions he asked me. After about a thirty-minute interrogation, he had an officer take me to the detention center where they placed me in a cell with my friend. Both of us were a little scared, but each laughed at our stories we told the policemen. To think that we both told them that neither one of us had a middle name was great! It wasn't even a part of our ill-conceived incomplete plan.

It took about two hours for my mom and dad to arrive. Yes, we did eventually tell the cops who we really were not too long after being in the cell, so they contacted Peniel and our families. My mom just yelled at me, exclaiming she couldn't understand why I would do such a thing to her or Pastor Ken and Mrs. Melodee. I'm not sure why my parents even showed up but they probably had to by law to release me back to Pastor Ken. All I cared about was getting out of those stinky clothes and eating something. Before running away, I hadn't even thought about going to California, so I wasn't disappointed. It would make for a good story to tell the other kids, and maybe I'd look a little bit cooler to them.

We were released, then immediately taken back to Peniel. Since it was a Sunday, all of the students were at our little church Peniel owned in St. Paul. Since I still stunk, I was more embarrassed than anything when we got there. Mrs. Melodee didn't even spank us! Instead, our humiliation was to wear these old, ugly, atrocious dresses that had been donated to the school. They were about forty years old, something your grandparents would have worn long, long ago. For the girls, wearing a dress to church at Peniel was mandatory, so we had no choice. Also, our punishment was to have to stay awake the rest of the day even though we didn't sleep at all the night before. The one-hour ride back to school that evening was pure torture since they wouldn't let us sleep until bedtime.

Life at Peniel had a way of giving you chances. There were chances to learn from your mistakes, and opportunities to travel if you improved personally and got good grades. Remember when I first saw the students at that little church with my family? Well, they were on a short tour at the time.

Tours were when Pastor Ken and some of the students would travel all over the country and tell people about Peniel and its mission, trying to encourage them to donate regularly to the school for our daily living needs. I remember one time when Pastor Ken left for a tour out west with three vans full of students, the gas tanks filled up, and then had only $20 left! They were gone for six weeks and came back with cash in Pastor Ken's pocket! God was very good to him. It might have something to do with the fact that even before they turned the key in the ignition, Pastor Ken would pray for their trip. He had huge faith in God, and it paid off in so many ways.

I was able to go on many of these tours. Since I had some musical abilities, Pastor Ken asked me to play either the piano or the guitar when they would sing. In the spring, the students who were doing well in school were allowed, if they chose, to go on the western tour for six weeks. I went on this tour three times during the five years that I was at Peniel. In the fall, there was a northern tour that went around Minnesota, Wisconsin, and Illinois. I went on all of these. What an amazing experience to see all of these places and witness the people sharing their homes and food and lives with us because they so strongly believed in what God was doing at Peniel. Lives were being changed and these stories of redemption were being shared during the testimonial portion of our services. Adults would weep for joy as they heard the individual child's story about how God had given them the opportunity to become something never thought possible before by either them or their families. The best testimonies came from counselors who had at one time been students at Peniel and received the help they needed, later experiencing the joy of becoming more involved in the ministry by becoming a counselor for the other kids in need of similar help. Eventually, that became me.

After I had been at Peniel for about one year, my dad called and asked me if I wanted to come home for the weekend. Now, I had been home only two times in that first year, and they were for Thanksgiving and Christmas. Those two times did not go so well - there had been arguing, yelling, me hiding out in my room to avoid them, etc. *So, why was he calling now?* When I mentioned it to my boyfriend David, he immediately said, "No way, don't do it." He was very concerned about what my dad might do. He knew that dad had sexually molested me. I told all of my friends about it. I told the counselors about it, but naturally, they didn't believe me. I was known for my lies. But now, my dad was calling up and asking me to come home for a weekend. I was very suspicious. I reluctantly agreed to go since I wanted to believe so badly that he had changed like he said he had and didn't want "that" from me anymore.

Dad arrived late that Saturday morning. He picked me up in his pickup truck, and we drove back toward the Twin Cities where we lived. It was only about an hour's drive. I asked him where mom and my brothers were, and he told me that they were at the cabin. *Had I made a bad decision?* Along the way, he decided to take me shopping. *Wow! Mom rarely took me shopping.* She bought most of my clothes, and typically I wouldn't wear any of it because I didn't like any of it. Dad's offer sounded very appealing but weird. At K-Mart, I tried on several dresses, and he bought me a couple of them.

Stranger yet was when he offered me cigarettes during the drive home. I didn't smoke! Both he and mom smoked all of my years growing up, and I hated it. I begged them to quit, and even after many promises from them to do so, they didn't quit. *So, why the offer?* Perhaps he figured that I was at the age where I might want to try it or something. I turned it down.

After we bought the dresses, he stopped at a liquor store. I had never been in a liquor store before and didn't know much about alcohol, except for dad's nasty beer and my parents' stash of lime vodka on chipped ice in the freezer downstairs–which I liked but they didn't know it. At school, I had heard kids talking about alcoholic drinks, and had heard about some wines. Dad turned to me and asked what kind of wine did I want? *What? How would I know?* This was really getting bizarre. I no longer trusted him at this point. His behavior was not normal. I had to tell him something though so I said the only name I could remember—Pink Zinfandel. He bought a jug.

We drove home. My mind was racing with uncertainty, questioning myself and my decision to be here, wanting desperately to go back to Peniel and be with my friends and David. We walked into the house and I stood at the top of the steps trying to decide if I should go downstairs to my room or go straight across to the kitchen. I began walking downstairs with my stuff when dad told me that I didn't have to sleep down there. I could use mom's bedroom, which was also his. *No way,* I thought! I tried to tell him that I really didn't mind sleeping downstairs, but he insisted on me sleeping in their bed. I only hoped that he wouldn't be in it too. I took my bags down the hallway into their room. Fortunately, he didn't follow me. Instead, he went into the kitchen and got something to eat, then opened that jug of wine. I tried to stay out of sight in their room, but he came looking for me since he wanted me to try on those new pretty dresses for him. That sounded harmless enough. I put them on, modeling each one for him, but changing in the bathroom. All I could think about was how do I make this situation not uncomfortable, and act as though I did not suspect that he would try and take advantage of me. I changed the atmosphere by wandering around the house and seeing what updates my dad had done. I went downstairs and saw the row of guitars that mom used to teach her guitar lessons. I took one of the acoustic guitars out, started to play it, and mentioned how I wished I had one. Strangely enough, dad said I could take that one.

The wine had begun to have an effect on him, and I knew what was coming. After I reluctantly agreed to have a glass of wine and chugged it, I told him I was exhausted and needed to go to bed. He said goodnight and went into the family room. I went to the master bedroom and acted as though I fell asleep on the bed while listening carefully to all sounds that would indicate trouble. It was about thirty minutes later when I heard him coming down the hallway. Pretending to be asleep, I laid there on my stomach, facing away from the hallway light. *Would he figure out I was awake or was he too drunk*? He walked into the room and stood at the foot of the bed. He quietly called my name. I didn't reply. He called it again. I must have been sleeping pretty hard not to hear him! I lay there. He climbed on the end of the bed and reached for me, trying to roll me over and remove my clothes. I just acted like I slightly awoke and rolled back over, mumbling something about "go to sleep." He tried again, this time more forcefully. By now, he must have known that I was pretending because he said he knew I was awake. *Then why was he trying to do this to me?* My father, my dad, was trying to have sex with me, his daughter! I wasn't his real daughter, but he had adopted me and raised me. I started to cry, which I think he noticed because he gave up and left the room. I just lay there, sobbing into mom's pillow.

The next morning, I woke up not sure what to expect. I tried to sleep as long as I could since I hadn't slept well the previous night, but it was time to get up. The house was strangely quiet. Dad hadn't slept in the bed. I tiptoed down the hallway, waiting for something to indicate where he was. I heard nothing. Walking around the house, I soon realized he was gone. I looked in the garage to discover his truck was gone too. Oh boy. *Now what?* He didn't leave me a note or number where to reach him. It was Sunday morning. His work wasn't open. So, I called Peniel and asked for David, my boyfriend. One of the counselors got him for me, and I told him that he had been right about not trusting my dad. David said he'd be picking me up in an hour. That's when I decided to hit that wine bottle. I had never been drunk before, that I remember, and now was as good a time for it as any. I cranked up the heaviest, most rebellious rock music I could find on the radio, emptied that jug of wine and danced myself into a frenzy. I soon passed out on the couch.

It must have been about 11:00 am when I awoke to the sound of pounding on the front door. David had told one of his counselors about my predicament, so they came to take me back to school. I was so tired, miserable and drunk, yet my hero had rescued me. We drove back to Peniel, where Pastor Ken and Mrs. Melodee questioned me about my behavior. Why had I been drinking, and why was I lying about my dad and his activities? Where did I get the guitar? After trying to convince them otherwise, they sent me to my room with the promise of calling my mother. Good, I said! She needs to know about it anyway! Of course, when they told her what I claimed had happened, she didn't believe it and told them that I lied about the guitar. I later learned that she did wonder about the possibility of my dad's supposed actions. You see, when he arrived later that Sunday morning at the cabin where mom and my brothers were staying for the weekend, he had babbled about having been a bad boy.

The following year, when I was fifteen, a counselor woke me up earlier than usual one Monday morning, informing me that my mom was on the phone. Let's see, I could probably count on one hand how many times my parents called me at school in five years! This was highly unusual. When I got to the phone, mom told me that my little brother had died on Sunday. She then explained that he had been in an accident on Thursday at a camp for handicapped children. Apparently, an electric golf cart that had been transporting a young boy from one location to another by two staff members had been momentarily parked. The staff had gotten out for a minute, leaving this boy alone. He managed to activate the pedals, causing it to lurch forward, and into a group of other children. The golf cart then rammed into my brother's wheelchair, and the impact sent him and his chair under a picnic table with the golf cart coming to rest against the table. Upon immediate inspection, the only physical injuries were scrapes on his knees, but there were internal injuries as well. He was having difficulty breathing, so he was rushed to the hospital, where they discovered a collapsed lung and other complications.

He died on Sunday during yet another surgery. The funeral was the following Thursday. I was able to attend his funeral and sat with my family. My little brother's life had impacted so many during his fourteen years! His twenty-five surgeries, seven years of hospital stays, and his physical handicap didn't affect his zest for life. His smile, which was very infectious, and his positive attitude brought joy to so many. He had been my six-million-dollar brother, with the heart of an angel.

On a cool fall night at Peniel when I was sixteen, I had a very vivid dream. In my dream, it was nighttime. I was sitting outside of the girls' house alone on the front steps and looking towards the big boys' farmhouse. The moon was bright so I could see the outline of the building. All of a sudden, I noticed two shadowy male figures running out of the house, and they took off down the long gravel driveway toward the county road. I watched them for a couple of minutes. Then I looked back at the house, and in an instant, there was a loud explosion and flames shot out of all of the windows, high into the sky! The structure of the house stayed intact, but no one else came out. I was stunned and horrified. Then I woke up. The next morning, I told this dream to a few of my friends and my counselor. She didn't know what to make of it. At breakfast time we learned that two boys had run away during the night. They made it to a town about thirty miles away where they made a complaint to the Sheriff about some students at Peniel who were gang members and had been beating them up. This would cause the State to take action and attempt to remove us kids until an investigation could happen!

About two hours later, since Pastor Ken had been alerted to this pending situation, he removed most of the students and took us across the state line to our church in the Twin Cities so that the state of Wisconsin could not get to us. Several Sheriff's vehicles did show up at Peniel. They took the few remaining students whom Pastor Ken trusted to leave there and told the staff they needed to shut down the facility until their investigation was complete. *Wow. My dream was unfolding in front of me!* Now the state didn't have any say in what Peniel did, as long as it was legal. We were not a government-run or funded facility. We were privately owned and operated on private donations. Needless to say, the state had to protect the kids and dispersed the ones they picked up into foster homes until their parents could get them. The rest of us who had been removed beforehand were given the opportunity to go home as well until the matter was resolved.

I chose to move home during this time. I hadn't lived at home for over three years! Many things had changed. James went off to college, my younger brother had passed away, Dad worked more, and mom kept herself busier than ever. I had changed too. The significant difference for me was now I had a personal relationship with the Lord. This meant I had to forgive my dad. I recall he and I were driving home one day when I brought up his past behavior. He was quite sheepish, embarrassed, and didn't want to discuss it. He did not speak about any of it . . . none of the details or explain why he had done what he did to me. But I told him that I had forgiven him for abusing me, and I truly meant it. For me, pain and awkwardness were no longer there between us. It was in the past. He began to cry and thanked me. *Wow did it feel good to forgive*! There were still a lot of emotional scars that I had to deal with though, and that would take a long, long time.

When Peniel reopened three months later, I was back there in a heartbeat. Life at home had proven to be too difficult for me, and for all of us. None of us could relate to each other, and I missed my school family and boyfriend terribly.

Since Peniel's property of seventy-seven acres was located out in the Wisconsin countryside, not in the city, we had septic tanks for sewage and propane tanks for the gas. Naturally, this led to many unforgettable events, especially in the winter. If our pipes froze, we couldn't flush our toilets or take showers. We would have to improvise. For water, we would melt ice in a large pot on the stove (that is if we had gas) to wash our hair in the sink or clean the dishes after meals. For bathroom needs, we had two options: you could go outside and use the outhouse, and yes it was a real one we nicknamed "The Moon," or you could use the large black pot with a lid that sat on the bathroom floor. Every morning it was the responsibility of two girls to carry this full, heavy pot way out into the corn field and empty it. Not an easy thing to do when the ground is covered in three feet of snow.

If we ran out of propane, it would get extremely cold in our house. I recall on several occasions waking up in the morning and seeing our shampoo frozen in their bottles because they were near the windows. The windows would have three inches of ice coating the corners and bottom. We could see our breath too. Each of us had to learn to adapt and often rough it.

People were always looking for ways to contribute to our school. The local grocery would let us come and pick up all of the produce that was starting to age. They would give us the dented canned goods, and often give us meats too. Many elderly women would donate their time and resources to make quilts for the students, and on those cold nights, we were very grateful for them, often using three quilts each just to stay warm. Neighboring farms would donate older horses for the kids to ride and learn how to take care of. Others would donate their time and help out with building repairs and upkeep. Weekly we would receive bags and bags and bags of used clothing. It would be like Christmastime going through them and getting new clothes and shoes. Men would help out maintaining the many vehicles that we had. There were multiple vans, station wagons, cars and trucks with several 100,000 miles on each of them from our many U.S. tours and trips to the Twin Cities.

Besides the thousands of people who prayed for us, the biggest contribution to the school had to be the money. Without it, there would be no Peniel. Back then, it cost about $700 a month to take care of each child. Now, it would be closer to $2,500. Pastor Ken only asked the students' parents to pay what they could afford, and the rest would be covered by love offerings and donations. My parents could only afford $100 a month, so we counted on people who believed in what the school was doing to pay the difference. It was a good thing that Pastor Ken was a man of faith. He prayed daily for God to provide in every way for each one of us, including financially, and God did. This was perhaps my biggest lesson learned. God will provide for those who are in need and ask for His help. Until He does, use wisely what you do have.

In 1983, Peniel Christian School opened up a second facility in Onarga, Illinois, at an old military academy that had been vacant for a decade. The group of people who owned it allowed Peniel to lease the property from them for $1 a year. Profit was not their goal, but rather to keep their buildings up and running by being occupied and maintained. There was a sports building, which had an indoor swimming pool and locker rooms, and two separate gyms, one of which had an upper track for jogging. We made good use of that entire building! There was also a two-story schoolhouse, an auditorium where we had our church services, and a dormitory that had four floors of bedrooms and a commercial kitchen with a dining room. On the outer perimeter of the complex was an old house where the academy's Colonel used to live. I don't recall us using this house.

I moved down to Onarga during the summer before my senior year. By now, I was a junior counselor and had gained a lot of trust from the staff. My boyfriend David also moved down there and was a junior counselor as well. We had grown very close over the years, with the knowledge that we were one day going to be married. We were quite the couple. The students looked up to us, usually respected us, and we were given privileges because of our status. Yes, we were even allowed to go on dates away from Peniel! It was during this year that I learned of David's troubles and addictions. He had been taking the boys out and letting them get drunk, getting himself drunk and being very irresponsible. As a result, he got kicked out of Peniel. They asked him to leave, at least until he could get his act together. Since he was eighteen, he agreed. I was heartbroken! Learning about his recklessness and weakness made me very angry. I hoped he could get his act together so that we could still one day get married. Time would tell.

on my own

It was in February of 1984, my senior year of high school when we had just begun our western tour. We stopped in a small town in Minnesota called Fergus Falls to perform at a Lutheran church where there was also a private Christian high school called Hillcrest Academy, a Bible college and seminary. One of our former counselors had been a student at the Bible college and had recently moved back to this town. I am not sure how this came about, but within twenty-four hours of arriving, I was given the opportunity to move out of Peniel and attend this high school, finishing the last three months of my senior year. The school was very expensive, yet the staff of Hillcrest and Pastor Ken agreed to allow me to attend with some kind of scholarship. It all happened so fast! When the tour group left the next day, I surprisingly remained behind, no longer a student at Peniel where I had been for nearly five years. I was on my own now. What a shock it was to learn how to be a person in the real world, the outside world where music, make-up, and television was a part of everyday life. I could now wear shorts, swear if I wanted to, go to movies, get a job, dance or do anything that I wanted to do! It took me a few months to figure out how to act, because I wasn't sure who the real me even was yet.

During this discovery phase of my life, unfortunately, I did learn something at this school that wasn't healthy for me. I found out that a new friend of mine had a bad eating habit of binging and then throwing it back up. I watched her do this, although she didn't know I was there. I didn't know about this before. This disorder called bulimia was a horrible, nasty thing. She believed she had a weight problem so she would deal with it by pigging out, then throwing it back up shortly afterward so that none of the calories or fat would get processed. This way there was no weight gain, and actually, she was able to lose some weight. This was entirely disgusting to me, but it planted the idea in my vulnerable little brain. I had been dealing with self-esteem issues since, well, forever. I viewed myself as merely average, sometimes as just plain ugly with my big nose and dark circles under my eyes, and with my big ol' backside. The problem was I loved to eat and to eat fast. Well, this bulimia gave me an opportunity to eat a lot and not have to deal with the consequences of it! I quickly began this lifestyle. I didn't always intentionally overeat, but if I did, then I had an easy solution of throwing up. This kept my weight down too, which helped my self-esteem. If I was angry or upset about something, then binging and purging was my way of dealing with it. Afterward, I would feel terrible about having done it, and often cried because of my weakness, but this pattern continued, and it continued regularly for the next fifteen to twenty years. Even to this day, I, on a rare occasion, still consider this as an option. But, the difference is I now know of the serious health-related consequences of living this way.

Graduation came in early June. I had sent an invitation to my parents, but all I received back from them was a card of "Congratulations" with $10 inside. *Wow. Now that hurt deeply.* It wasn't the small gift that hurt, but rather the fact that they wouldn't even come to my high school graduation! (Apparently, they weren't involved in the decision to send me to Hillcrest in the first place, nor were they even aware of me being there. It was when they got bills in the mail, along with the invitation, that they found out.) Regardless, I was graduating, and they wouldn't come! Again, I felt so very alone. My former girls' counselor from Peniel, Rene, and her husband Eric, lived in this small town and were my only contacts with my former life. They supported me both financially and emotionally while I was at Hillcrest Academy, and they were my only friends or family at the ceremony. No matter. I knew that life is what you make of it. The road ahead was wide open and up to me. I had no one else but the Lord, and that seemed to be just fine. He knew the way for me, and I was determined to find it and follow it.

After graduation, I stayed in Fergus Falls and got two jobs. The first job was a full-time Certified Nursing Assistant (CNA) at Broen Memorial Nursing Home during the graveyard shift. The pay was low, but I didn't need much. It was my first job, and I enjoyed helping these elderly people who didn't seem to have much family either. I also worked a part-time job at the local mall in a little shop called Dixie Donuts. Between the two jobs, I stayed out of trouble and learned how to make my own way in life. I rented a fully-furnished basement apartment from a sweet elderly lady, Ms. Elvina Balkan. I bought my first car, a brown '74 Comet, and was given a thirty minute lesson on how to drive a stick-shift by the salesman. Then I was on my own.

After about one year of life in Fergus, I was ready to make a change. My old boyfriend David had turned his life around and was back at Peniel as a counselor. Oooh! This information caused me to pray briefly about such a change, and after speaking with Pastor Ken and Mrs. Melodee, David was at my door helping me pack up. Off to Peniel I went again . . . this time as an adult counselor for the girls.

It only took me about four months to figure out that David wasn't being faithful or honest with the school or me. He was again allowing the boys to drink and smoke pot while they were out with him. It caught up with him though, when Pastor Ken found out about it. He was once again kicked out, this time for good. There were no more chances for him there. I too kicked him out of my heart with a good slap to his cheek when I learned of his other relationships. This was the end of my first love affair.

My time at Peniel as a counselor ended a few months later as well. I felt God leading me in another direction . . . to Kansas City.

CHAPTER 5

Kansas City here I come

Kansas City Youth For Christ (KCYFC) was a multi-faceted ministry that I had become aware of as a teenager. This ministry had a heart for youth, and they reached them in many ways. There were two ranches for kids to attend during their summer break where they could stay for one week or as long as the whole summer. There were fantastic activities for the kids to enjoy, including swimming, horseback riding, ping pong and trail bike riding. The intention was to lead kids to Christ while learning that being a Christian, though challenging, can be fun too.

During the fall, the ministry sponsored Bible clubs in public schools. These Bible clubs helped encourage kids to live out their faith with the support of Christian classmates as well as to extend an invitation to join the clubs to their friends who didn't know Jesus. They also had Saturday night youth rallies where hundreds of kids could come for two hours to sing uplifting songs, listen to speakers from all over the country, hang with their friends, eat at the snack bar, and ultimately make lifelong decisions for Christ.

KCYFC owned a non-profit television station that would air positive programming for all ages, ranging from the pre-taped Saturday night youth rallies, kids' cartoons, women's talk shows, and various church services, all Biblically based.

For those who wanted to further their Biblical education and get more involved in the youth clubs, there was a nine-month intense training on campus called Christ Unlimited Bible Institute, where students would go through the entire Bible in nine months, learn how to preach in front of others, and learn how to work with the youth.

When I was a student at Peniel, we had a volunteer basketball coach who was also involved with KCYFC. When he showed us a film about the summer camps, I immediately knew I wanted to go, but didn't see how. I had no money and had doubted Pastor Ken would allow it. Much to my surprise, I was allowed to go as long as I was a worker at the ranch which would pay my way. So, during the summer between my sophomore and junior year, I went for one week. This was by far the most significant experience of my teenage years! Never had I seen so many kids and had so much fun! I worked hard in the kitchen though. The following summer I went back for three weeks, working either in the kitchen or the snack shop which allowed me access to all of the fun activities as well.

Fast forward to my time as a counselor at Peniel, and I am praying about my future. I am twenty years old. Remembering the excitement and great times I had at camp, I felt led to move to Kansas City to work at the camps for the summer and then see about possibly attending their Bible School in the fall. I knew if I did this, I would be moving away from my family (not that we ever saw each other) and would need to address them one last time, perhaps mending fences. My future had a purpose, but I couldn't proceed without talking to my family.

I called home, and mom answered. I told her I was moving away, but that I needed to see them before I left. She agreed to meet with me at the house but mentioned that my brother was away at college and Dad needed to be at the cabin. They would not be home when I was visiting. Up until this point, mom and I hadn't had much of a conversation longer than five minutes, so since it was to be just the two of us, I felt anxious. But on the day we met, we both had open hearts and minds and actually talked face-to-face, heart-to-heart, for six hours! I spoke freely about my hurts and disappointments regarding them sending me away, not visiting me, not coming to my graduation, and yes, I told her about dad. This time, she believed me! We cried together, we hugged, and we loved each other for the first time in so many years. It was a day of deep healing for both of us. The information about the incest led mom to conclude it was time to divorce my dad. She explained that his behavior for so many years was extremely unusual, but by describing to her what he had done to me, it began to make sense. She put many puzzle pieces together that day. It is unfortunate that my revelations would lead her to the decision to divorce dad, but I had not been there for so long I didn't understand what she had been going through either.

I thanked her for choosing to send me to Peniel because it did take me away from an abusive dad and it gave me the opportunity to accept Christ! The Lord knew what He was doing when He had them send me away. Mom told me that no one else from her side of the family seemed to understand though. For those of you who doubt my parents' decision and are angry about it and can't find it in your heart to forgive them, then take it up with the Lord God! He was the one who directed my parents to send me to Peniel! I doubt that if I had continued living at home that I would have made it to adulthood, either emotionally or physically. I would have gone down that destructive road of drinking, drugs, and sex to alleviate the pain in my heart. Perhaps I would have even considered ending my life again. Fortunately, I do have a heavenly Father who could foresee the future and knew then that what I needed was a new life, and a new family at Peniel. For mom, learning how I felt about this both hurt and healed her. To this day, she struggles with their decisions. It is often harder to forgive yourself than to forgive someone else.

I moved to Kansas City, Kansas, in the summer of 1986, and spent the next two months working at the youth camps as a girls' counselor one week at a time. It's interesting how God used my past experiences to help some of those girls. Many had similar situations of abuse by their fathers, uncles and older male family friends. I had no idea that incest was so common and could hurt so many! One girl was even raped and chose to keep the baby! The biggest struggle was helping these girls learn how to forgive those who had hurt them. Many of the girls were already Christians, but had painful experiences that scarred them both mentally and emotionally, and didn't know how to heal or work through these memories. Others needed to learn how to move forward in a healthy way. Much of it boiled down to forgiveness. I had to deal with that when I was 16. It had taken a few years of maturing both emotionally and spiritually to learn the importance of telling my dad face-to-face that I forgave him. I did just that. I honestly believe in my heart that I had done so. That's not to say that we can trust that person not to continue to make that same mistake again or with someone else. The one who hurt us may not want to change their behavior patterns. Our job is to forgive and use wisdom when dealing with them. It helps us to heal when we release them from their actions against us. It certainly helps when they seek our forgiveness and do a complete 180, but that is not always the case. This is what so many girls at camp were struggling with. I thank God that He allowed me the chance to encourage them and pray with some of them about forgiving their transgressors. That summer had a significant impact on me in many ways.

In the fall, I attended Christ Unlimited Bible Institute, affectionately known as C.U.B.I, the one-year (nine month) Bible School and Youth Missions training ministry of KCY-FC. When you are a student at C.U.B.I., you cannot have a job for income, but instead you are a missionary-in-training, and therefore have to raise your own funds. Monthly I mailed out a newsletter to family and friends, updating them on what I was doing and what God was doing in my life. Ironically, none of my family supported me financially. However, God did provide for me in many ways! He connected me with a young Christian couple with three little children who let me live in a downstairs spare bedroom for $100 a month. Also, since I needed transportation, I was able to borrow an old '67 VW Bug from a family that wasn't using it at the time, but a few months later they took it back since they were moving away. Well, to my surprise, someone anonymously bought it from them and gave it to me. *Wow! Never had I experienced such a gift!* God certainly answered that prayer.

This green Bug, though free and now mine, had everything wrong with it that could possibly be wrong. For example: the wipers lasted only a couple of minutes, so if it was raining, I would have to reach out of the window and literally squeegee it. The engine, which was in the back of the car, would slip from 1st gear into 3rd gear, causing me to pull over and have to reset it while it was revving super high. One day while I was driving, I heard a loud noise that sounded like I had blown a tire, but the car didn't drive any differently. I pulled over, and after circling the car, looked underneath and noticed that the battery had fallen through the floorboards due to extreme rust, and was dragging on the ground! I had to strap that battery onto a couple of 2x4's just to get around! Due to the car's lightness, several of my classmates and friends on numerous occasions would, as a gag and for fun, move it, sometimes sideways in between other cars, and sometimes to a totally different part of the parking lot, making it hard for me to find it. Oh, and they TP'd it too. They had more fun with my Bug than I did! Needless to say, my little car lasted the rest of that year until I could afford to buy a newer car. The Lord made sure that was covered too.

Every month there seemed to be a check or cash from an anonymous person that got me through to the next month. Looking back, I still can't believe that all of my bills were paid, I had gas for my car, food for my table, and enough money left over for personal supplies! The Lord used many of His people to help me get through this time. Truly this was a miraculous year for a young missionary in training.

As we neared the end of Bible school, each of the sixteen students had to decide what area we were going to within the ministry, or whether we were going to move on to something else. Up until this point, I felt as though my training and history of working with kids was leading me to the high school clubs as a youth leader. Something just didn't seem to feel right about it though. I eventually began doubting that youth work was my calling. Perhaps He wanted me to venture out into the mission field of Russia or Africa! The notion of smuggling Bibles into Russia, or the hope of living within a tribal community that had never even heard the gospel, let alone seen white people, had been on my heart for some time too. One night I got face down on the floor in my little basement bedroom and poured my heart out to God, asking Him to show me where He wanted me to go and what He wanted me to do. I remember very clearly an overwhelming sense of direction, as though a voice had said "Television." I had met a few people from Channel 50, their TV station, and had toured it since it was a big part of the ministry, but I hadn't really considered it as a contender for my future. However, now I knew without a doubt that this was where He was leading me.

KYFC-TV 50 became my new family for the next three years. I began in their tape library, putting away the 2", 1" and 3/4" tapes, and then setting up the programming shelves for the next day's shows. I learned how to schedule the Public Service Announcements (PSA's) and the Emergency Broadcast System (EBS) tests. I learned how to make dubs of the shows by transferring them to VHS tapes. They taught me how to run their cameras in the studio for their live and pre-taped shows. I even helped do make-up for some of the guests. I think my favorite part though was acting for their live telethons. We would dress up as different characters depending on the theme of the telethon and help in that way to raise funds for the station to continue operating. Some of my most memorable roles were being a Swiss clockmaker and a firefighter. One time they spun a young man and me around in a commercial-sized dryer! No, it wasn't turned on. They manually rolled the back of the drum to flip us around a few times on stage. For the Saturday Night Youth rallies, I was a regular camera operator. This gave me the opportunity to help out afterward with any kids who wanted to make a decision for Christ or needed some counseling in an area that I could assist with. It was a learning and growing time for me, both spiritually and personally.

Every year while I was living in the Kansas City area, I moved into someone else's home. For the first year after C.U.B.I, my good friend's mother, Hazel, and her husband invited me to live with them. Since her daughter Shari and I were buddies, that sounded awesome, like an extended sleepover! She and I got to spend a lot of time together, and her mom became like a mother to me. She counseled, challenged, encouraged, scolded, and loved me in spite of my many faults. Her compassion for me and my situation deeply affected my life and how I viewed motherhood. Hazel loves her Lord, and is to this day as beautiful outside as she is inside. She remains a key figure in my life.

The second year a widowed lady and her teenage daughter had a large spare room above their garage that they rented to me for $200 a month. For me, this was like an apartment with a girlfriend. The daughter Cheryl and I became friends, and at that time I really needed one. A few months later at Christmas time, I met the lady's son, Brad, who was usually away at college, and sparks flew. We began a long-distance relationship.

When Brad had spring break, I even went down to Santa Fe, New Mexico, and spent a few days with him. I began to have hope that this guy might be my future husband.

The KCYFC Saturday night youth rallies would draw all ages, not just the high-school kids. College students, adults and even a few elderly would come to hear some good preaching and great music. These two-hours rallies were highly anticipated each week, since the musicians brought in were well-known. Big names like DC Talk, Carman, Truth, Dino, Larnelle Harris, Steven Curtis Chapman, and the Gaither Vocal Band headlined the events. The speakers were also just as fabulous, like Richard Kiehl who was the actor who played "Jaws" in two James Bond films, comedian Mark Lowry, John Ankerberg, and Josh McDowell.

During that spring, I became friends with another young man named Shannon who frequently attended the rallies. *Now, this guy was cool!* He was a very tall guitar player in a Christian rock band and had fabulous long hair to match. After my friendship with Shannon began to deepen and my feelings for him began to grow, I had to make a decision about who to date. I had been dating Brad for about six months now, and I liked him a lot, but I chose the guitar player. Shannon's outlook on life was more in-tune with mine.

Shortly after we began dating, I needed a new place to live. It had become an emotional struggle for my former boyfriend Brad's family to have me living under their roof when I had ended my relationship with him. So, Shannon's kind mother invited me to move in with them in a spare room since he was living out on his own. I excitedly agreed and lived there for a few months. The irony here was that one day his mom and I were telling each other about our families, and discovered we had family in common in Minnesota. I learned that my boyfriend and I were actually related! It was quite the stretch of distant cousins, and besides, I was adopted, so it didn't really matter. But, it is funny to think that I was dating my distant cousin. It was during this time that Shannon decided to move to Nashville to further his music career. It was tough to see him go since we had been together for nearly six months. So I thought it would make sense for me to follow him there. After all, we had been talking marriage! This decision ended my four years in Kansas City.

I have never been the kind of person who tucks my tail and runs home when something goes terribly wrong. For one thing, I didn't have a home to go back to. For another thing, what was there for me back in Kansas City? When someone follows a boyfriend across the country, or even just down south, one should expect life to change dramatically and prepare for anything. What I wasn't prepared for or expected was for us to break up three weeks after I arrived in Nashville. I should have known that since Shannon was now a traveling musician, that his life was changing as was he. He had new places to go and new people to meet along with other young women. I was holding him back. He wasn't ready for what I thought we had. Genuinely heartbroken, I resolved to find myself a new man in this new city. I had already gotten involved in a popular church named Christ Church, with many young Christian musicians and roadies, and soon felt confident in my prospective options.

I had to get a job fast. The money I had saved up for the move was quickly running out, as was the patience of my two room-mates. They had been trying to encourage me to get out there and earn my keep. It wasn't long before they asked me to move out, even though I had just started a new job as a wait-ress at Applebee's. I had never been a waitress before. I had no idea how to deal with people who drank a lot, not to mention I didn't know anything about mixed drinks. This was all for-eign to me. It was the first time that I was truly out in the real world, no longer protected by that umbrella of fellow Chris-tians who spoke as I did, acted as I did, and dressed like I did. I was now out of my comfort zone! Anyone who has waited tables before understands that you get a wide variety of cus-tomers, ranging from businessmen to families with children, to singles wanting to hook up with someone, often with their eyes on you. I will say that this experience in my life helped me realize how difficult it can be to be a waitress and earn the customer's tip, and it showed me that every person comes in with their own problems of which we are unaware. Some-times just an honest smile for that person, or perhaps giving them their space would make their day a little brighter. There was a reason that God put me in this position, and I tried to make the most of it for a year and a half. I did move out of the girls' apartment and into an efficiency apartment—one room with a bathroom, borrowed a couch from a friend, bought a $100 bedroom set I painted black and a few basic cooking sup-plies—and settled into my first place by myself.

Applebee's was not my only job at the time. Obviously work-ing at a restaurant does not guarantee you a good monthly income. I also got a part-time job as a long-distance telephone operator at Sprint. This only lasted for a few months though due to layoffs. Additionally, I worked with a friend at a catering company for a brief time. Needless to say, I didn't earn a lot of money at any of these jobs.

Alone with no boyfriend or family nearby, it was at this time in my life that I thought about finding my birth family. I had minimal information, just a few details which mostly came from my adoption papers and from my uncle's investigative work. I knew I had a sister about two years older than I was and that her mother was overprotective of her. I knew that I had lived in Sioux Falls, South Dakota. I had a grandfather who had been a Baptist pastor. I knew I had been adopted when I was two years old and that my birth family had given me up, primarily because the mother didn't seem to like me as much as she did my sister, her other daughter. I didn't have much when my new family adopted me and was not very healthy. I also knew that my name had changed when I got adopted, and I remembered reading what it had been. Not having a sister in my life, I made the decision to find my real sister.

Knowing my birth father's first and last name which I got from the adoption papers my mom had, I called information in Sioux Falls, South Dakota, and asked for any listing with his name, Andrew Matson. Surprisingly, there was only one. *Oh boy.* Now my heart started beating hard. I gathered up courage and dialed the number. A woman answered the phone. I said, "Hi. I am looking for your daughter." She put her husband on the phone. He answered, "You looking for Melissa? She is living in Colorado Springs now. Do you want her number?" I answered, "Yes." He then asked me what school we attended together. Well now, I didn't know the name of a single school there, so he had caught me in the lie. I answered him by saying "sorry" and hung up. Now my heart was pounding, and my hands were sweaty. He had told me her name at least. I called information in Colorado Springs and asked for this Melissa, but no listing came up. A dead end. This meant that if I wanted any more information about my family, I would have to call them back and tell them the truth! It was time to call my mom for some good advice. She proceeded to tell me that I needed to call them back immediately, apologize for deceiving them, tell them who I really am and that I believe they are my birth family. About 30 minutes later, I found the courage to do just that.

I redialed their number, but this time Andrew the dad answered. I told him that I had just called a few minutes ago asking for his daughter, but that I had lied to him. I was not a friend of hers. "Actually, I called because I think you might be my birth family," I said. He was silent for a second . . . and said, "That's impossible. We never gave up a naturally born child for adoption." *Huh? So, what, was I hatched? What an odd thing for him to say!* He then hung up. I sat there, stunned, for what seemed like hours, not knowing what to do next. *They denied having me. They DENIED having me!* I had hit a painful dead end.

I don't think I would have made it through those difficult days if it hadn't been for my friends, Sidney and Elaine. Elaine and I had met at a club where my former boyfriend Shannon's band was playing. We hit it off immediately, and joke to this day about meeting at a bar. Sidney was a friend I met at our church, Christ Community. She and I decided we should get an apartment together, just south of downtown Nashville in the L.A. area, otherwise known as Lower Antioch.

My desperation to find a Christian man who wanted to become my husband proved futile. I had met so many prospects, had searched in every corner of singles groups' gatherings, had joined gyms, had hung out with guys from various Christian bands, had visited different churches, all the time eyeballing each guy as a potential mate. I dated cowboys, military men, college students, bodybuilders, musicians, roadies, and even a model. None of them shared my enthusiasm for getting married! Well, at least not getting married to me. At the "old" age of twenty-five, I gave up. I made the decision to stop looking. If there wasn't a man for me, a Godly mate, a best friend, then maybe the Lord wanted me to be single. *Perhaps that was my calling? Could it be that I was not meant to be married?* Knowing that was now a distinct possibility, I honestly quit looking for that special man. I gave my future back to the Lord. He was once again in charge of my life. It was only when I made that conscious decision, that the Lord revealed to me that I had already met the man.

getting married

I can still remember how I felt the day of my wedding, walking down the aisle, alone. Alone: a statement of my life to that point. Independent. My decision to walk alone down the aisle stemmed from not having a dad who was man enough to join his daughter on the most important day of her life. His decision to take a vacation with his new wife to Las Vegas to avoid any unpleasant confrontations with my mother proved to me what his priorities were. Thankfully, my mother was there. Mom had recently become a pastor, but due to her pastoral duties several states away, she didn't arrive in town until the wedding rehearsal. Actually, I knew she would come, but had hoped for some help from her in preparation for my big day. *What can one expect, though, when there hadn't been much of a relationship for the first twenty years of my life, and two of those didn't count because she wasn't even my mother then? Anyway, since my dad wasn't going to be there, then who would walk me down the aisle?* I considered the only other male that had been in my life for so many years, and that was my older brother, James. Except, we hadn't really spent any measurable time together since seventh grade when I was sent away from home.

Alas, my choice to walk down the aisle alone was due to having been basically on my own since I was thirteen years old. After discussing it with my fiancé Drew, we agreed it was natural for me to go on this journey alone. He would be waiting at the end of my walk, thus ending my twenty-six years of solitary life.

Drew had been my knight in shining armor now for nine months. We began dating the day after Thanksgiving in 1991, while he and four fellow band guys lived together in the Big House.

The Big House was formerly a movie distribution house for Christian films. The only windows were in the front of the house, in the kitchen, the offices and in one bathroom. The rest of the big house had concrete floors with tall ceilings that had been painted black, paneled walls dividing the remaining four windowless bedrooms, a large viewing room with several rows of those vinyl covered chairs you would find in old movie theaters, and a control room with 10' x 5' windows that overlooked the old viewing room, which the guys had converted to their rehearsal room. The lack of windows allowed the guys a great night's sleep at any time of the day since it was pitch black in their rooms. You could hear your roommate's snoring two doors down the hall since the walls were not insulated. In any case, this rock-and-roll bachelor pad came in handy for "Wanabam" since they would have some very late night gigs. Wanabam, an acronym of the band members' last names, consisted of Drew who was the keyboardist, his younger brother the drummer, and three other friends whom they had invited to join them in Nashville, Tennessee in 1989. Of course, five musicians living in a large rental house attracted lots of attention from both girls wanting to be their "friends" and from guys wanting to be their buds. Yes, I did become one of those girls.

At the time, my good friend Sidney and I had started hanging out with the bass player of Wanabam. We all attended the same church, Christ Community Church, in the quaint little town of Franklin, Tennessee, which is just southwest of Nashville. He and two other guys from the band went to this same church. The bass player, Sidney, and I would go to movies together, play ping pong, go out to eat and just hang out at his house, the Big House. Darts were a big pastime for the band in their house. The guys had set up a dartboard in the main hallway and would have these tournaments that could go on for hours! The paneled walls had thousands of little dart holes in them. Many of us girls would sit there and cheer on our favorites. It was during these games that I began to take notice of the keyboard player.

Drew, the keyboardist, was a rather quiet guy, coming across as a little shy. He was funny and cute but looked too young for me. I recognized him from our church, too. Naturally, I dismissed him as a potential boyfriend because I thought he was about four years younger than me. Everyone knows that girls mature faster than boys, so I figured he just wouldn't be ready for a relationship like I already was. (It was around this time that I had given back my dating life or the lack thereof to the Lord.) So, it took a few weeks before I finally asked one of his bandmates how old Drew really was. Was I surprised to hear that Drew was actually more than two years older than me! *What? Wow.* Now I began to look at him differently. Perhaps he would be a good catch. Soon I was cheering him on as my favorite dart player. To my surprise, he acted like there might be a spark of interest for him too. I would catch him looking at me. He then challenged me to a game of darts, and of course, he won.

Shortly after this, the band had a show at a local bar for Halloween. Drew invited me to go see them play, so Sidney and I dressed up in fun costumes and went. When I saw Drew dressed up as a pirate with his long hair in a ponytail, saw him rocking out on the stage, and saw his big smile when he looked at me, it all made my heart jump. I was beginning to fall for this guy!

I was mesmerized by his musical talents. He was writing and composing a song for *Keyboard Magazine's* current songwriting contest. I would describe Drew's style as jazz meets funk, pop meets blues, and rock intertwined with them all. When he played his completed song for me, he had this boyish grin, the look that one has when he's just realized how much his performance has affected someone else. I complimented him on his talent, hoping it wasn't too obvious that I was quite taken with him.

The day after Thanksgiving, my friends were all busy or with their families, so I got this crazy idea to call Drew and see what he was doing. When Drew answered the phone, I could hear several other people in the background laughing and having a good time, which made me more nervous because I really wanted to be there with him. Drew asked how I was and what was going on. I told him I that I was fine and not doing much... so he invited me to join them for a barbecue. His mother was in town visiting for the holidays, which meant that I would get to meet her as well.

The next thing I remember is walking in the front door and being greeted by my prince! He led me into the TV room where they were all gathered, and he introduced me to his mother. Seeing her, I felt as though I was looking at a mirror image of what I would probably look like at her age. She looked so much like what I envisioned my real mother to probably look like as well! If I didn't know better, I would have thought *she* was my real mother. Quite overwhelmed by this feeling, I immediately went over to her and hugged her, saying how great it was to meet her. She appeared genuinely pleased to meet me. It felt right. The whole scenario just felt right, as though I was finally home.

I stayed at the Big House all day, playing darts, eating, listening to music and gabbing with everyone. Drew's younger brother was there too, along with his new wife. Some of the other band guys had come back from visiting their families, and we all hung out into the night. By 9:00 pm, Drew and I found ourselves sitting in the TV room, watching television alone. This room was just off of the kitchen and had a couch, some chairs, and a small television stand. It was chilly in there too, but I wasn't about to complain. Drew and I finally had some quality time together . . . alone.

We started talking about ourselves, sharing many things that were pretty personal too. The evening went on, and the conversation got more deep, more intense. At one point, I remember thinking that this could be the man I would marry! Never had I been quite so taken with someone so quickly. The whole time we were together was so relaxed, comfortable and easy. So, just to see how much he could handle, I told him about my childhood. I didn't hold anything back. He learned about my adoption, my growing up and getting sent away to boarding school, but especially about my dad and the incest that occurred with me. Drew didn't get up and say "good night" or laugh, or even appear in any way to doubt me, so maybe he wasn't too freaked out! He listened intently to every word I had to say. That is when I knew he was my future husband.

We stayed up until 3:00 am that morning, getting to know each other, hugging, holding hands, and sharing many things. Years later when I brought up that night to Drew, I asked him how he felt after I disclosed my deepest darkest secret. He said, "I was scared! I had never heard of such things and wasn't sure how to react. I didn't think that I would marry a girl with such a messed up family. I always pictured myself marrying a girl with a normal family life as I had." Fortunately, God had other plans.

The following day, Saturday, was another opportunity for me to hang out with Drew and his family, which consisted of his newly married brother Derek and his wife Desha, and of course his mother, Janet. His father, older brother, and sister were not there since they lived in Florida. Drew had invited me on Friday night to join them Saturday for a movie matinee. We decided on the thriller "Cape Fear." Not your average family movie! It did allow me to sit very close to Drew though, and due to the intensity and proximity, we held hands. I'm pretty sure his mom and brother noticed too. There was one part of the film that bothered me a lot, and Drew noticed it, probably because I was squeezing his hand so tightly. The scene with Robert DeNiro being inappropriate with Juliette Lewis in the school auditorium had hit too close to home, and an observant Drew tried to reassure me that it was all going to be OK. Yes, with him by my side, I knew it would.

Sunday we all met at our church for the late morning service, which many of the young adults our age typically chose to do. Janet Wiseman had joined Drew and Derek that day, so I got to say my goodbyes to her after the service. She then flew back home to Florida, promising we would see each other again soon.

You could say that my and Drew's dating relationship was already in full swing after our first weekend together. Within two weeks, we had both admitted to each other that we were in love! *Wow*. At the end of the first month, Drew had told his family that he thought I was the one, much to the chagrin of some family members. It was too fast for them. His sister, his brothers and his friends called him with doubts. Yes, it was fast, but when you know, you know! I knew, he knew, and that was that. We couldn't easily convince some of them though. I'm sure they said things like, "Time will tell," and "We'll see." Many thought we were simply too different from each other for it to work.

We had only been dating for a couple of weeks when one day as I was doing my laundry at the apartment's laundry facility, someone had the nerve to actually steal three pairs of my pants and some undergarments! Drew showed up shortly after this happened and saw how devastated I was since I only had two more pairs of pants and very little money to buy anything. Amazingly enough, this was another day that he proved he was my knight. He gave me some money and took me shopping to get a couple of new pairs of pants. *WOW!*

My old, orange Mazda hatchback was dying and was no longer reliable. When I had been dating Drew for only one month, he went car shopping with me. We found a brand-new blue Toyota Tercel for $7,000, and he actually co-signed the loan for me. Now that certainly caused quite a stir in his family!

We had been dating for about two months when Drew told his father that he was going to propose to me. I would have loved to have been a fly on the wall that day! Apparently, Mr. Wiseman was OK with it because he purchased a set of rings for the engagement to show support for his son. (I was unaware of this purchase until much later.)

My belief that Drew was going to propose soon led me to start guessing the scenario. *Would it be Valentine's Day? Would it be during our trip to visit his family in Florida? Could he hold out until my birthday in April?* I hoped not but was willing to wait if that was how long it would take him to go through with it. At the time, I was still a waitress at Applebee's Bar and Grill. Ironically, I worked just a half of a mile from where Drew and his brother both worked, Pearl Drums. Pearl Drums, one of the largest drum companies in the world, has their U.S national distribution center in Nashville. Drew and Derek would both come to Applebee's for lunch, sometimes just the two of them, other times with freight reps who were trying to schmooze Drew for business. Once in a while, Drew would come alone. But, always he would wait to sit in my section so that I could serve him. Not that serving him was my highlight, but rather hanging out with my handsome boyfriend and sometimes his brother, who often were mistaken for each other. It must have been the hair. Both had long, thick, wavy big hair. Drew's hair was pretty close in length to mine at the time, down to the middle of our backs.

Valentine's Day came with high expectations of a proposal from Drew. I told all of my regular customers that I anticipated getting engaged that night. Naturally, Drew and I had arranged a date night for the evening. He picked me up at 6:00 pm, and we drove to a very nice seafood restaurant, L&N Seafood. When we got there, we discovered that everyone else in town had developed the same craving for fish that night. After putting our name on the waiting list, we waited and waited, for nearly two hours. To me, it didn't matter much because I was with Drew and he might propose tonight!

We were finally seated at an oversized table for two. It was covered in a white cloth with a lone candle in the middle of the table. We ordered dinner and wine, then began to talk while we waited anxiously and hungrily for our appetizers. I recall quite vividly how Drew seemed rather nervous. I was so anxious for the big event that I started to tell him of how I felt about our relationship at that point. He got this frightened look when I told him that I had initially thought he wasn't really my type, and that I truly enjoyed his friendship. I wasn't done though. I then informed him of how deeply I felt, and thoroughly loved every minute that I was with him. You could see this sigh of relief come over his face! I didn't mean to scare him but instead wanted him to know that I did truly love him. After a wonderful meal with more intimate conversation, we returned to his car, a white 1989 Dodge Colt. Now my curiosity was taking over, so I took a quick peek around, trying to find something that would give away his proposal intentions. When I started to open the glove box, Drew quickly asked me what was I doing, snooping around in his car! Well, of course, I was looking for a box with a ring in it. Yes, I told him of my suspicions. He laughed it off, wondering why I would think that there would be a ring in there? I did see the paper bag though. I knew it!!

It was a chilly rainy night, but we decided to drive down to the riverfront anyway. It was a good night to live on the edge, so we parked on 1st Avenue. After he got something out of the glove box (the paper bag), we began strolling down the sidewalk in the light drizzle. The only light was the yellow glow of the street lamps that lit our way. The Cumberland River was to our left, down a steep hill. There didn't appear to be anyone else around, most likely due to the rainy weather. I had on a dress and heels, and Drew was wearing his coat.

We walked for about ten minutes without an umbrella, taking our time while we held each other closely, both for warmth and intimacy. He stopped walking at a small cluster of benches under the golden glow of the city streetlights lining the river walk. He turned me to face him and took hold of both of my hands. *Here it comes,* I thought! Drew started by saying that he had never expected to find a girl like me and that it scared him to have such strong emotions of what had to be love. I didn't notice the cold or the rain anymore. He said a few more sweet things, and got down on one knee, and asked me to marry him. *I knew it!!* I asked him if he was sure about this. With only a brief hesitation, he said, "Yes." I looked at the ring in that yellow light and smiled big. "Yes!" I answered. He had proposed! I was going to get married! Someone loved me enough to want to be with me forever. That was a miracle. *Thank you, God!*

We decided to have a fall wedding, so that meant we only had about six months to prepare for it. Neither one of us had very much money at all, nor made much money, so we knew that our wedding was going to be small and without much extravagance. There were to be two maids of honor and two best men. We invited about 100 people, and about seventy-five showed up. This was the perfect size for our wedding.

Our families lived in different states than we did. My parents and extended family still lived in Minnesota, and Drew's parents and two of his siblings lived in Florida. So, getting them all to Nashville, and getting them to attend and be joined as a family, proved to be a difficult task.

The big day arrived. It was August 29, 1992. We had dated now for nine months and were ready to embark on our journey of marriage, with the honeymoon immediately following the ceremony. Drew's family was in the travel business, so arranging an eight-day trip to Switzerland proved to be rather simple, though not cheap.

As the *Wedding March* played, I started cringing, not because I was getting married, but because the brass quintet that I had chosen to perform at our wedding was terrible! *Did they really practice?* Perhaps the real reason I am blushing now has nothing to do with the groom or my emotions. The fact that most of our friends were in the music business might have had something to do with that. *Ugh.* This was a part of our wedding we will never, ever forget.

Nonetheless, I kept walking down the aisle, looking at our friends to see if they were snickering or merely ignoring the music. I'm hoping they are just watching me as I walk alone. I can see Drew's eyes on me, and the softness they are showing calms me. I finally make it to him. *Good, that horrific sounding music finally stopped.* The Episcopal priest, Drew's father, then begins his words of wisdom. His assistant is my mom, a Lutheran pastor. Talk about two completely different people! His father regarded marriage as a holy, sacred event to be taken very seriously. My mom saw marriage as a joyous day of celebration, the union of two in love for life. This made for a very interesting ceremony and an even more interesting marriage of families.

After our honeymoon in the quaint mountain town of Grindelwald, Switzerland, Drew and I rented a house in a southeast Nashville area called Berry Hill. This house was tiny. The funny thing is that it was right next door to the Big House where Drew had lived for two years with the band! Living in the little two-bedroom house gave Drew easy access to his bandmates next door, and privacy with me in our house. Surrounding us were many houses that had been converted into small businesses, such as music recording studios, dance studios, yoga studios, and film houses. We lived in this house for three years until the owners decided they wanted to move back in. So, off we went with our 30-day notice to find our first home!

We looked at small ranch-style homes that were in our meager budget and found a house. We paid $96,000 for a ranch with an unfinished basement which was also where the garage was located. It had three bedrooms and two baths. It had a very large and beautiful park-like backyard with approximately 100 trees, and a wide creek that flowed along our back property line. The whole property was nearly 1.25 acres, and it was ours, all ours! Our mortgage was just over $700 a month, which was less than our previous rent. For the two of us, this house and its setting was absolutely perfect, for the next year and a half. During that time, life had some big changes in store for Drew and me!

finding my families

It was November, 1995, and I was twenty-nine. We had been married for a little over three years and were happily living in our new brick ranch home. I had just started a new job at a television production company, and Drew was still at Pearl Drums.

We began talking about my birth family again. I so desperately wanted to know about them and to find my sister. Drew and I were thinking about starting a family of our own soon, and knowing my parents' health histories was going to be a major factor. I told Drew about the time I called my birth family, the Matsons, and had lied to them but I got my sister's name. "Well," he said, "Let's try that again." However, this time *he* would pretend to be my sister Melissa's friend from school and get her phone number. We took a deep breath, and dialed. Andrew the dad answered again, and this time it worked! My former father gave Melissa's phone number to Drew! Now, this was exciting. We actually had something to work with. Since we had a copy of my adoption papers with their names listed on them, there was enough information for us to share with my sister and perhaps get reacquainted!

My sister Melissa was about two years older than me. She had been an only child since I was given up. So, surely when we speak, she will be just as excited as I am to find her sister! Nervously I dialed her phone number, and she answered. I said "Hi. You don't know me, but I believe you are my sister." She did not believe me since she was too young to remember any of it, and because her parents had never told her about me nor brought me up in conversation. I informed her of my adoption papers that had her parents' names listed on them and how they had given me up before I was two years old. These facts intrigued her enough that she asked me to fax a copy of it all to her so she could read it over. I did just that. She confirmed that she had received them, and after a quick review, told me that she would discuss it with her parents during Thanksgiving, which was just a few days away. To have been a fly on that wall! I waited for her call the day following Thanksgiving break, and when she didn't call me, I called her.

Melissa said, "Yes, you *were* my sister. But, you are *not* my biological sister. My parents adopted you several months after you were born. They decided to give you back since they didn't think it was working out. I'm sorry that I'm not your sister." Silence. *What?* I was *floored.* She then told me how upset her mother was at me for contacting them and asked me never to contact them again. Melissa did say that I should get in touch with the adoption agency for further information. Then, she was gone. Drew and I just sat there, stunned. *What can you say after that?* However shocking this was, it did explain what her father meant when he told me they had never given up a naturally born child. Now I had to start the search all over again, but, for whom?

Drew and I were both determined now more than ever to find my real birth family. The fact that I just learned of my second adoption and of another family out there stirred up more curiosity and intrigue. *Who were my parents? Did I have any other siblings? Why was I given up the first time? What's their story? Who am I?* With earnest, we began the search.

The next day, we got in touch with the adoption agency, Lutheran Social Services, in Sioux Falls, South Dakota. That was where I had been born, given up, adopted, given up again and adopted again. LSS was the company that handled it every time. They told us that we had to get a court order to open the adoption file. This had to be done through the County Court Office by the Clerk of Courts. We had to send a letter to the presiding Judge petitioning for three orders regarding my birth and adoption:

1. An Order releasing the court file
2. My original birth certificate
3. The complete adoption agency file

This letter also had to include my known date of birth, adoptive parents' names and dates of known adoptions. We mailed all of this December 6th.

On December 12th the presiding Judge of the Circuit Court sent us a letter noting receipt of our request. She also told us of a scheduled hearing set for January 22nd that we need not be present for, but we had to notify three agencies about it in case there were any objections to our securing the information in the files. We wrote to the Department of Social Services, the Catholic Family Services, and the Lutheran Social Services, and informed them of the pending hearing. We then sent the Judge another letter stating we had done so. On January 22nd, no one appeared in court to contest our receiving the files, so the Court Order went through.

For the next couple of months, I anxiously waited every day for the mail to arrive. Finally, on April 6th, I received a package from the Department of Social Services in South Dakota! In it was a letter stating receipt of the Court Order and the information they had on file. They were forwarding the order to the office of Vital Records, Department of Health, and they would be in contact with me regarding obtaining a copy of my birth certificate. I immediately scoured the new papers for some clues as to who I was.

I read an eight-page document all about my history from birth to being adopted the first time, to details about why they eventually gave me up. I sat there dumbfounded as I read my mother's reasons for giving me back. She indicated that from the beginning she had negative feelings toward me because she didn't like my chin. Although my chin did improve over time, she never got over this initial feeling. She mentioned several other reasons for not keeping me: I had dry, scaly skin; I screamed a lot when being given a bath; I had piercing screams to show discomfort rather than just crying; I fell down a lot and landed on my face with no attempt to protect myself; I had short legs and poor balance; she was never able to just play with me because I wasn't cuddly nor would I permit her to hug me; I would eat anything including sand or whatever I could get my hands on; discipline didn't sink in;

I didn't sleep through the night; I seemed sensitive to light; I wasn't willing to chew my food and would eat a quarter of a peach whole; and I wasn't toilet trained yet (at one-and-a-half). *Wow. I must have been a terrible child!* To think that at such a young age, I could affect this woman so much. I think it says a whole lot more about her than it does me. Thank you, God, for getting me out of that house!!

This document also gave me what I had been searching for all along: my birth name. I was born as Kimberly Sue Davis. My birth mother's name was Ruth Elizabeth Davis. My father's first name was Russ. No other details were listed about him. Finally I had clarity!

The information that was missing now was how to find my mother's birth family. I had names and places from thirty years ago, but who knew if anyone still lived in Sioux Falls, South Dakota, or Fargo, North Dakota, where my birth mother's family had lived. It showed that my maternal grandfather had been a pastor in Fargo. So, now we needed a listing of churches. This wasn't readily available via the internet yet, so we contacted the Chamber of Commerce in Fargo and requested an area directory with church names and numbers. We received that in the mail about one week later and then began calling churches in Fargo. When we asked the third church on our list if there had ever been a Pastor Davis who served there, the woman responded, "Yes." She then said there was a parishioner in their congregation who remained a friend of the Davis family and that she still kept in touch with them. The receptionist then asked us if we wanted her number. With heart thumping, I replied, "Yes! Oh yes!" On April 15th, we called Esther Abernathy.

Esther had been a friend of the Davis family for about thirty-five years. She knew them before I was ever born. In fact, she was one of only two people outside of the immediate families who even knew I existed! This was not a mere coincidence. This was obvious divine intervention! When Esther answered the phone, her initial response was one of concern. She wanted to know why I was looking for them? What was my intention? She was not willing to give out their phone number or any other critical information until she could reach them first and get their permission for me to move forward. She asked me to call her back the following day. The one piece of information that she did share with me that day, sadly, was that my birth mother had died. She died when she was 19 in a tragic car accident. I began to cry. *Why did she tell me this now?* I would have rather heard it from my birth family, but knowing this now I would have time to digest the news, realizing I would never get to meet her, at least in this lifetime. That was my whole purpose for trying to find my family! Well, I can't stop now. I needed to speak with her parents, my maternal grandparents and find out what happened so long ago.

When we spoke with Esther the next day, she told us that my Grandpa William was ecstatic to hear that I was looking for them, but that I would have to wait a few more days to actually speak with him. He was heading out to a pastor's retreat for four days, and we had to wait until Thursday evening to call. She gave me Grandpa's number in Portland, Oregon. The wait was exhilarating agony.

On Thursday, April 20th, 1996, when I was thirty years old, Drew and I gathered in the hallway of our little ranch home with a pad of paper and a pen, and I dialed Grandpa's number. I hit "record" on our telephone's answering machine.

Ring, ring . . . ring . . . ring . . .
"Hello," he answered.
"Hello, is this Mr. Davis?" I asked.
"Yes it is," he replied.
"This is Kari Wiseman calling," I said.
"Well, Kari, pleased to hear your voice! Let me get my wife on the phone, ok?" he asked.
"OK," I said. His voice was kind, but he spoke loudly and slowly.
"Gail (I heard him say), this is Kari. Ohhh, Kari. What should we say about this?" asked Grandpa. He was noticeably choking back the tears.
"I don't know," I said. *Man, was I nervous!*
"Hello," Grandma said as she got on the other line.
"This is Gail," Grandpa said.
"Hi, Gail. How are you all doing tonight?" I asked.
"We're doing fine. We got the call from Mrs. Abernathy from Fargo, and I think she got back to you obviously," said Grandpa.
"Yes. She was very nice. She was very helpful," I said.
"Well, I understand you've made a real effort to find out about your birth mother. Is that correct?" he asked.
"Yes, it is," I said.
"What can we help you with Kari? We'll just chat. We'll just talk. Feel very free. I want you to know that we have no problem with you calling us or asking, I want you to know that," he said.
I replied, "I appreciate that. I don't want to make it difficult or weird or anything like that. I don't want to intrude on you,".
"You're not gonna sue us for a million dollars?" he jokingly asked.

"No," I chuckled back.

"Or 10 million dollars?" he continued.

"Pastors don't make that kind of money," Grandma chimed in. By now, we were all laughing about the mere thought of me trying to sue them. That thought NEVER ever crossed my mind. Why would I? They spared my life!

"I promise I won't sue you," I said.

For the next forty-five minutes, we spoke openly and honestly about what had transpired in our lives. It was just brief nuggets of truth that we each needed to get this relationship started, to make us all feel a little more comfortable with this process of getting to know one another. He shared how "Ruthie," my birth mother, had gotten pregnant out of wedlock—the result of a one-night stand with a seventeen-year old boy—and for the final few months of her pregnancy, she had gone into seclusion in Sioux Falls to have the baby. They shared details of her life that were comparable to mine. She was a good student, but she could have been a great student if only she would have applied herself. She loved animals, the outdoors, and was quite witty. She was 5' 3" tall, had blue eyes and sandy blonde hair. They shared that when she was eighteen, she had moved out to Portland, Oregon to live with her sister Grace, and get a job. The two of them, along with Grace's fiancé, were traveling home for a four-generation family reunion on December 18, 1969, when Ruth hit a patch of black ice in Montana, and they skidded off the road going over a 242' embankment. Ruth was thrown from the car, breaking her neck, but Grace and her fiancé were only moderately injured. Ruth died on the way to the hospital from internal injuries just one week before Christmas. There were more than 400 people at the funeral, and they received more than 500 sympathy cards. My note pad at this point was soaked with tears. Grandpa William shared about Ruth's other siblings. She had two older brothers, Dave and John, in addition to Grace. Grandpa came from a family quite small in stature. His father was only 5'3", and his mother was only 4'10". Grandpa himself was 5'7", and seventy-four years old. Grandma Gail was seventy-five. They had been married for fifty-four years. I had a German and Scottish heritage.

The conversation took an unexpected turn when Grandpa asked me where we lived. I told him Nashville, Tennessee. After more conversation, he began to tell me of their next family reunion that was planned for June, just two months from then, and that it was to be held in Pigeon Forge, Tennessee. That was only a three-hour drive away! He said he wanted to talk to his kids about it, but he thought maybe we could join them there and we could all meet! *Whoa.* Never had I expected such an invitation! To think that they are scattered all over the country, and they planned their reunion unknowingly so close to where we lived! Grandpa and Grandma, Grace and Bob, and their two kids lived in Portland, Oregon. John and Dawn and their one son lived in Omaha, Nebraska. Dave and Sherry and their two kids lived in Jacksonville, Florida. At this point, I must say again that I do not believe in coincidences. God works in mysterious ways and has a reason for everything! So, their planning of this trip so near to us was by His hand. He knew what was to be, although none of us did. *How could any of us have known?*

We spoke for nearly an hour. Drew sat next to me during the entire conversation and read over the notes I had been jotting down. Afterward, he and I hugged, cried, and read the notes over and over, letting it all soak in. Unfortunately, the tape recording stopped after about thirty minutes. But, Grandpa had told me he was going to call the other family members and ask them how they would all feel about us joining them at the reunion. When he called us back several days later, he told us that it was a unanimous decision of "YES!" I was overwhelmed with emotion.

Less than two months after I spoke with my Grandfather for the first time, we were on our way to meet the entire Davis clan, all eighteen of them. It was only a three-hour drive, but it seemed like an eternity! My aunt had mailed us a picture of the family's last gathering and had written down their names, so Drew and I passed the time driving by trying to memorize who was who. The Davis family had rented Walden Lodge— a huge lodge in the Pigeon Forge area with a couple of small cabins on the property. They figured Drew and I would be more comfortable staying in a cabin near the lodge since this was our first visit and none of us knew each other yet. We agreed that this was a good idea (just in case they were really weird and we needed an escape). When we arrived, we were warmly greeted by several members of the family, but a few of the guys were out playing golf. The women helped us get settled in our cabin, and then gave us a quick tour of the massive lodge. There was a game room with foosball, bumper pool and ping pong, a dart board and board games. This was going to be fun! There was an industrial-sized kitchen, a large dining room and sitting room, and two floors with seven bedrooms. Outside there was a large swimming pool with a diving board. Drew and I were ready to dive into this family, weird or not!

By the time the men returned from their golf game, we had gotten out the adoption papers and notes that we had acquired the last seven months and were sharing them with everyone. It was also media day since everybody had to take pictures of me and we took pictures of them. There were pictures of Ruth brought out and I brought some of me from when I was young so we could compare features and physique and discuss personality traits. The next two hours were just a meet-n-greet for all of us, and Drew and I felt extremely welcomed.

That evening after dinner, the gang decided it would be fun to sit together, and have everyone tell something about themselves. We each shared personal stories of growing up, getting married, memories of Ruth, and dealing with the sadness of her death. When it was my turn to share, I took the most time since there was so much to share about growing up, my many years at Peniel, and how I found them after all these years. When Grandpa shared his stories about Ruth—her getting pregnant and then dying, we were passing multiple Kleenex boxes around. This sharing time was truly a time of deep healing for the entire family since Ruth wasn't spoken of much after her death. It was such a painful topic that everyone had kept their hurts and thoughts to themselves for years! Ruth had died on her way to a reunion, and here I was, her daughter, at a reunion twenty-seven years later. *Who would have ever thought that?!* We stayed up that night, talking, laughing and crying until 3:00 am. I will never ever forget it.

As I mentioned before, Drew and I brought with us the adoption papers that we received over the months. There were about forty pages total from various agencies and personnel. These were poor copies of the originals, and often it was quite difficult to discern the words, so someone had taken the time before sending them to us to review each page, and with an ink pen, fill in those extremely hard to see or read portions. I took out these documents—which seemed like gold now—and shared them with my Grandparents, aunts and uncles, and even my cousins. Everyone wanted to read them. Between the papers and our conversations, Drew and I learned quite a bit about Ruth, her one-night-stand, her pregnancy with me, and my first few days of life.

Ruth and Russ had been set up by a mutual friend in Fargo, North Dakota. This one-time encounter resulted in her getting pregnant in the fall of her sophomore year of high school. She was only fifteen. The two families—the Davis' and the Walkers—met privately to discuss the situation, and my grandparents concluded that the whole pregnancy was to be kept very quiet and no news was to be shared with anyone else. Russ's family, the Walkers, were not given further updates on the status of Ruth's health or her child's. Since Ruth's father was a pastor, it was decided by the Davis family that she should go away for the last couple of months of her pregnancy so as not to draw attention to herself, which would have caused her father's church congregation to ask embarrassing questions.

On February 14, 1966, Ruth Davis was admitted to a maternity home in Sioux Falls, South Dakota, under the care of a social worker with Lutheran Social Services. Ruth opted to stay at the home under an assumed name, Ruth Dover. She remained there for two months. As the time of my birth drew very near, my future had to be discussed. The social worker wrote: "Ruth feels adoption is the better plan for her child because she is not ready to assume this responsibility at her age. Her parents concur with this decision."

On Easter Sunday, April 10, 1966, I was born and named Kimberly Sue Davis. The social worker wrote: "Ruth *avoided* seeing her child, in part, at least, because she was afraid she might be unable to leave it. She did not feel ready for this responsibility and felt that any decision she made to keep the child would be because she wanted something of her own. Ruth was mature enough to recognize this was not a good reason to keep her child. Ruth wept during our conversation regarding the type of home in which her child would be placed."

Ruth left the maternity home on April 15, five days after I was born, and the case was closed.

I did find in the paperwork a letter that Ruth wrote on May 16, 1966, to that caseworker. It was written one day after Ruth's 16th birthday. It says: *"Well, I am finally sixteen. I'm sixteen and have already had a baby. Doesn't that sound nice? How is Kim? Has she been adopted yet? Even though I never saw her, I miss her very much. I think of her quite often. I pray for her that she'll have good parents, grow up to be a nice young lady, not like her real mother and that she'll be a fine upstanding Christian. I hope she never turns out to be like me. I love Kim. I didn't before she was born, but I do now. I would like to see her and hold her, but I wouldn't want the responsibilities of raising my girl. I'm sure Kim will have fine parents, and I hope that she gets all the love that she deserves. Thanks for all your help. Write me about Kim please."* Ruth Davis

I shared this letter with the family, and Grandpa wept. He remembered these details like it was yesterday! He and Grandma chose to open their hearts and freely reminisce about their youngest child Ruth, recalling details that had been pushed deep down . . . details that had caused them great sadness, pain and even regret. They agreed that not all of the decisions they made were most likely the best ones, but none of that could be changed now. All we could do was go forward, looking back only to understand what had taken place, and how it made all of us whom we are today.

The next couple of days that we spent with the Davises were filled with swimming, eating, shopping in Gatlinburg and Pigeon Forge, playing games like foosball and ping pong, and just spending time together. It felt so natural to be with them! The beauty of this family was that all of them were born-again followers of the Lord like Drew and me! I couldn't have asked to be a part of a better family. I had five new cousins too, and I was the oldest. My cousins teasingly told me that I had become the new favorite grandchild. No contest. I was now at the top of that ladder! Seriously, they all knew that they were deeply loved by Grandma and Grandpa. I had just been missing, but now was found. By the time Drew and I left Pigeon Forge, we knew that they had adopted us into their fantastic family. I was loved! I knew we would keep in touch and see them again soon.

For Drew, the search, finding my mother's family and the reunion all touched him very deeply. It inspired him to write and compose a song about it, especially about my part of it. When we had the next family reunion, he played and sang it for the whole family, and there wasn't a dry eye in the house.

Here are the lyrics:

Without Ruth
It was 1950 when she came into this world
He called her Ruthie, she was daddy's little girl
She had a smile in her eyes, like an angel from above
And this child of his filled his heart with love.

In '65 his little girl was 15 years of age
That summer with a one night stand, her whole life would change
She wasn't ready for motherhood or a boy she hardly knew
And giving up her baby was the hardest thing she'd do

Without Ruth it wouldn't be the same
Without Ruth everything would change
Through the years and through the tears
He'd come to know the truth
Life would be different without Ruth

In '69 she moved away and was living on her own
A holiday reunion was bringing everybody home
But instead many tears were shed on that Christmas Day
While driving home she lost control and Ruthie passed away

Without Ruth it wouldn't be the same
Without Ruth everything would change
Through the years and through the tears
He'd come to know the truth
Life would be different without Ruth

It was the summer of '96 when her daddy's dream came true
A family reunion with the grandchild he never knew

She had a smile in her eyes like an angel from above
And now Ruthie's girl fills his heart with love

Without Ruth it wouldn't be the same
Without Ruth everything would change
Through the years and through the tears
He'd come to know the truth
Life would be different without Ruth.

My journey was not yet complete. I had to finish the circle. I had to find my birth father, though I honestly didn't want to. Dawn, one of my new Davis family aunts who was married to Uncle John, had asked me if I wanted to find him, and that if so, she knew how to get in touch with him. Dawn had a mutual friend from high school that both she and Russ kept in contact with. He was the guy that helped set up Ruth and Russ' original meeting with each other. Reluctantly, I agreed to let her proceed and get in touch with her friend.

In the meantime, Drew and I planned a trip to visit Minnesota in September to see my brother in the Minneapolis area, and my mother and her family out in the western part of the state. There were aunts and uncles and cousins Drew hadn't met yet since they weren't able to attend our Tennessee wedding. I also wanted him to see Peniel, and meet Pastor Ken and Mrs. Melodee, who had been so influential in my life and actually were like parents to me. The school was still operating, and I was quite anxious to visit after so many years, especially since it was only about an hour's drive from the Twin Cities.

In August, I received a call from my Aunt Dawn. She asked again if I truly wanted to find my birth father. After I confirmed my answer of "yes," she proceeded to get in touch with her friend of my father. The ball was rolling . . .

Ralph and Fern Walker were celebrating their 50th wedding anniversary on August 25th, 1996, with friends and family in Fargo, North Dakota, when their son Russell received a call from an old friend, Dan. Russell was not prepared for the news that followed. Dan told him that his thirty-year-old daughter was looking for him! Russell was not a married man, nor did he have any other children. He was surrounded by his family as they celebrated his parents' anniversary, and now he was being told that he had a daughter! He was totally overwhelmed. For years he had wondered what had happened to the child he created thirty years ago. He had been left out of any decisions made by Ruth's family and had never been told when I was born or even what gender I was. This news was the greatest news he had ever received. To sum it up, let me quote to you a portion of a letter he wrote to me merely one week after he learned of me: " . . . *I am thrilled to know I have a daughter. I have a daughter! How foreign that seems at times, yet it is so wonderful! I welcome you with open arms and an open heart. My chest swells with love, peace, and joy when I think of you and this flows out freely to all I com- municate with. God's love is embracing and healing us, and I celebrate it. I feel more centered and more whole than I can remember. I am more present as I release the deep anguish and sadness held for so long. I am being freed to stand tall in the light and love more . . . Today I am a rich man, and tomor- row I will be richer. Thank you for bringing more light and joy into my life . . .*"

We spoke for the first time three days before he wrote this letter. I learned that he was single, forty-nine years old, 5'9" tall and 145 pounds. The most amazing part was when he told me he lived in Minnesota in the Minneapolis area! *Wow*! That meant we would be able to meet him in three weeks when we went there on the trip we had already planned! Definitely not a mere coincidence, so God did good again. It's hard to believe, that within five months, I would have found and met both sides of my birth families! This was truly, truly incredible. My Lord had most graciously arranged this.

On September 14, 1996, Drew and I landed at the Minneapolis airport. It was to be a very big week! We rented a car and drove to western Minnesota where mom was pastoring, and where we spent the afternoon with my mom's relatives, including two uncles and their wives, several of my cousins and their children, and my grandma Elle, my mom's mother. It had been close to eight years since I had seen most of them. We went to our cabin on the lake, and on the way, we saw the world's largest twine ball! We also got to see where my brother worked as an engineer, and visited the Mall of America. The drive to Peniel was scenic with the fall leaves and the rolling hills, and Drew was able to see the beautiful Wisconsin countryside. Driving up that long gravel driveway at Peniel filled me with so many fond memories of growing up there. Pastor Ken and Mrs. Melodee were there as well as my former counselors, Eric and Rene, who had helped me out in Fergus Falls. What a great reunion that day! Now Drew could visualize where I had spent my youth and understand better why I appreciated Pastor Ken and Mrs. Melodee so much. Once we left Peniel, we drove back to the Twin Cities and went by the house in White Bear Lake where I grew up, and to my elementary school. Drew saw it all.

By the time we left, he had seen nearly every area where I had lived, except for Fergus Falls.

The September day I met my birth father was bright and beautiful. I admit that I was excited but nervous about it. I didn't want to find him for a long time. I was hesitant to do so. But, now that the day was here, I was ready. We drove to the house where he was staying and saw on the front lawn a pink sign that read, "It's a Girl!" *Was that about me?* We met Russell at the door, and he hugged me so tightly! He wept a little as he said, "Hi, I'm Russell." He did look a little like me! Our profile was similar, with our noses, mouths, and eyes. *Wow.* No doubt now that he was my father. For years I had thought Rod Stewart was because so many of my Peniel classmates tried to convince me that I looked just like him, but obviously it was a myth. Russell led us to the living room where he passed out pink candy cigars and had a pink banner hanging up with my birth weight, length, and married name written on it. He was so proud to be a father even if it was thirty years after I was born! We met his parents that day too, my paternal grandparents. Pictures and stories were shared. Quickly we discovered the same love for games, so they broke out the cards, and we all played a few hands. Russell, Drew and I went for a walk, took about a hundred pictures, and then we all went out to lunch and just enjoyed getting to know each other. It was truly a memorable day. It was a spectacular year.

My family trees were beautiful. Now it was time to add branches of my own and watch them grow.

Kari with her new brothers

Kari is adopted!

Kari's birth mother -
Ruth Davis

Kari's birth father -
Russell Walker

Kari - elementary school

Sharing testimony on Peniel tour

Peniel Christian School

Kari and David

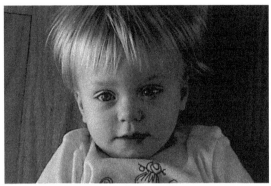

Daughter Karli

The Wisemans, 2006

Son Dane

Drew and Kari, 1996

The Wisemans, 2016

Bullfrog Bellows

Hangry Snake

Pastor Ken and Melodee Sortedahl, 2017

The Wisemans, 2018

branching out

To say that my life was now complete since finding my birth families would be close, but not accurate. Yes, God had given me the privilege of discovering, quite easily, two wonderful families whom I could now call my own. I had a loving husband, all of his family who now lived in the same city as we did, a brother and mother, who even though they lived far away in Minnesota still kept in close contact, and now my two birth families. I was loved. All that was missing now were our own little ones to love.

I admit to never daydreaming about being a mom and having children running around. You see, I was afraid that I would be a bad mother. I wanted to be a loving mother and be a good example to them. That wasn't exactly something I had been around on a regular basis. So how does someone love a child unconditionally? It would be a few more years before I would have to deal with those questions.

On Easter day in 1997, one year after speaking with Grandpa William for the first time, Drew and I decided it would be fun to fly out to Portland, Oregon, and spend the holidays with the Davises. Aunt Grace and Uncle Bob and their two kids lived out there, along with Grandma and Grandpa. What a great time we had! Bob and Grace put us up at their house, which sat on about forty acres atop a hill overlooking the valley and distant hills that surrounded their property. They had a Christmas tree farm too. We spent our days eating lots of food, playing Taboo and Guesstures, and visiting other relatives in the area. We took day trips to Seaside and Cannon Beach, Portland, Multnomah Falls, and Seattle. Spending time with this incredible family was indeed a blast and a blessing.

Back in Nashville of the same year, Drew and I moved to the west side of town and bought an older ranch style home. Now we had nearly two acres of land, another creek bordering our property, and about fifty trees. Mowing this beast of a yard took us three hours on a riding mower not to mention the time trimming and weed-whacking. It was worth it for us because the yard gave us a lot of privacy and space. The kitchen had already been remodeled and was bright and open, so we thought we'd never move again. After more remodeling a couple of years later by adding a master suite with a bath and a nice deck and patio, we had the nearly perfect house. There were plenty of bedrooms, if and when we had children.

It took me and Drew nearly a year to meet our neighbors who lived across the street from us. It happened when their pets got loose and came over to our yard to graze. Ponies. They had three of them living in their backyard, along with a cougar (that was caged), about eighty goldfish in a pond, a pig, a large noisy bird, and multiple dogs. With the new and unwelcomed "fertilizer" now in our yard, we walked over to their house to meet them. It turned out they were quite friendly. They told us that at one point they had six cougars, but they all eventually started dying from old age. Glad they had only one left when we moved in.

My dad, the one who had adopted and raised me, and his second wife were traveling around the country in their little RV. This was something the two of them enjoyed doing for their vacations. He called me, out of the blue, and asked if they could stop by and visit with us. Wow. I hadn't seen him since I was sixteen, and now some sixteen years later, he was reaching out! There hadn't been much communication between us in that time, partially because I had moved away from that area and relocated to various states throughout the years, and also because I had put that part of my life behind me. I knew my dad's new wife had three daughters. That part *really* bothered me. *Where did my responsibility lie? When I had learned of their marriage, should I have told her what dad had done to me, and would she have believed me? Maybe today she would ask me, "Why did I wait so long" to tell her. What if he had already been abusing them without her knowledge? What if he denied all of it?* In addition, he chose not to attend my wedding and went on a vacation with his wife instead, so I had some hurt feelings there. Drew and I agreed to invite them to visit with us, but I knew that I had to confront him about some things. We had never sat down and discussed any part of our past except for that one time as a teenager when I told him in the truck that I forgave him. That one-minute, one-sided chat didn't materialize into a heart-to-heart. It needed to happen. In addition, I was fairly certain that his wife had no idea of the incest that had occurred. *What man would volunteer that if it wasn't necessary?* His wife thought the reason I had been so distant from them was because they didn't attend our wedding. Nope. I wished it was that simple. Now it was time to inform her of the truth.

As I sat there on the couch with Drew, who was struggling with his own anger towards my dad, and as they both sat on the opposite couch facing us, I began to explain why I was distant. Yes, I was bothered by him not attending our wedding, but that wasn't the whole story. I told his wife everything: specific details of my childhood sexual abuse. She sat quietly, visibly trembling. She then spoke up and asked me, "Are you sure of this? Could you be mistaken? Please tell me that this is not true." I could only answer, "I am sure." As I watched her reaction to this revelation, it was as though I was seeing someone's life destroyed right before my very eyes. Her face grew white, she was very quiet, and soon let go of his hand. She obviously didn't know what to do, or how to feel. She had doubts about my story being true. I then asked my dad why he did those things to me. This grown man, now sobbing, said he didn't remember any of it, none of it. The only recollection he had was the time he invited me home for the weekend, and that was just fragmented. He sat there, a broken man, not remembering any of it. *That just wasn't fair!* I had to deal with the consequences of the incest for so many years, wondering if I would be normal and respond to men in a healthy way, and he sat there, claiming no memory! His wife was so overwhelmed with emotion that she left the room for a few minutes. When she returned, she explained to me that my dad had been dealing with a serious case of memory loss—long term and short term—for some time. He wasn't able to hold down a steady job anymore because of it. He had other health issues too and therefore needed regular home care. She was that caregiver for him. Dad then asked me for forgiveness—something he had never ever done before. The fact that he was asking for forgiveness, for acts he claimed no recollection of, was a bitter pill to swallow. I had already so freely given it to him in years past, so how could I withhold that from him now? In the Lord's eyes, there was no longer anything to forgive. Other than his lack of memory, I had nothing else to forgive. But, dad had to ask for it for his own sake, trusting me that this great ugliness had occurred, believing that he had done these horrible things to his own daughter. With my heart beating wildly like that of a racehorse, and knowing in my heart that the past had been dealt with, forgiveness was again readily given, but this time, it was for his sake. Now I had to let go of the past completely. That meant not dwelling on the pains and memories. Forgiveness means to completely forget what happened, and throw it as far as the east is from the west, not to bring it back again, just as the Lord does with our own sins when we beg Him for forgiveness. I knew now that I could put the whole thing behind me. Soon after my revelation to dad's wife, she decided it was time for them to go, and mentioned that they had a lot to talk about. They drove away a short while later. I learned after a few months that his wife chose to forgive him for what he had been and had done in the past, believing in her heart that he was a new man. She is a remarkable woman. I have no knowledge of any concerns or problems occurring between dad and his stepdaughters.

For more than five years, I had been working for a television post-production company, Music City Digital (MCD), which was owned by High Five Entertainment. I was their Operations Manager and I absolutely loved this job. My role consisted of scheduling clients' offline or online editing times, videotape duplication, making sure materials were digitized in the proper editing bay, preparing clients' specialty baskets of goodies, ordering their lunch, and billing them when their jobs were completed. MCD was in the center of Nashville's Music Row area where recording studios, artist management, and small businesses were located. This gave us great access to amazing restaurants and other studios that we partnered with in post-production.

Drew and I had been married for eight years now, and still, we weren't pregnant. I began to question whether or not having children was in our future. We did enjoy the life we had, but also knew that if we never had kids, one day we would look back and regret not having them, or worse, be lonely from not having any grandchildren running around. I began to journal.

January 5, 2001 - Friday evening: I am awakened in the middle of the night by what feels like VERY bad PMS cramps. It lasts for about fifteen minutes, then I go back to sleep.

January 6-10, Saturday - Wednesday: Each night I get woken up by these extremely painful cramps in my lower-mid abdomen. Never have I experienced such PMS cramps before and have it last for so long! So, start my period already!

January 11, Thursday: I've had it. Sleepless nights, questions, concerns. *Why am I cramping so bad?* I scheduled an appointment w/ my family Dr. He is a little concerned as to what it might be since the symptoms don't add up to either an infection or pregnancy. So, he orders a urine test. I must wait until tomorrow for the results.

January 12, Friday: I am off today from work, though I did go in for a couple of hours. Impatiently, I start calling the Dr.'s office at 11:30 am. After four calls, finally at 4:15 pm, the Dr. calls me at home. Well, he tells me, it's positive. I'm pregnant! SHOCK! Now, Drew and I had been trying for about four months. Oddly enough, I had been sick over the holidays, so we were only together 1x that either of us can remember in that time period, and that was New Year's Day! *WOW. I'm pregnant!*

That night, both of us were anxious, nervous, and a little scared. I wasn't sure that I was ready to be a mom! This would be such a huge change for us! We sat on the warm bathroom floor (it was heated). This was it. It was real. This really is happening! We sat there, hugging each other in shock.

The doctor was still concerned about my cramping in spite of the good news. He saw me the next day, but now the pains were beginning to decrease, then subsided altogether. I forgot all about it.

I don't recall any other issues with my pregnancy other than needing to give up caffeine due to a history of arrhythmia, which is an irregular heartbeat. I abhorred the smell of garlic, which we typically used in most of our cooking, and mayonnaise was completely disgusting.

I had been at MCD for nearly five years when I learned that I was pregnant. At seven months of pregnancy, they chose to let me go. This was very traumatizing for me since I loved that job and didn't understand why they were firing me. We would also lose that income. It was a difficult time, with me asking God many questions about our future, my faith, and how we would manage.

On September 11, 2001, I was thirty-eight weeks pregnant and at home alone, watching the devastation of terrorism unfold on television minute by minute, worrying if I was going to go into labor early. Fortunately, I did not. Karli Belle Wiseman arrived a week later on September 19th, 2001. Now I had to learn all about motherhood and prayed that God would help me to be a good one.

My mom and brother came to visit us a couple of times in Nashville. When Karli was just two months old, even Grandma Elle, mom's mother came down. I enjoyed it when they would visit. Drew, being a wonderful husband, would give me all the time I needed to talk and play cards with them since he didn't like to play. He won many, many brownie points this way.

When Karli was a little over two years old, Drew and I took a Christmas vacation to Minnesota and Portland, Oregon, to see my two families. We spent the first four days with my brother and mom and her family in Minnesota, because Grandma Elle was very sick with cancer and wasn't expected to live much longer. It was a bittersweet visit knowing that I would probably never see her again in this life. We then flew out to Portland on Christmas Eve and stayed with my birth mother's family, the Davises. Christmas Day was filled with food and fun and extended family as usual at Uncle Bob's and Aunt Grace's house. We enjoyed many games with even more laughs. Someone took a picture of me with Grandma Gail in her dark purple suit. She was sitting in a rocking chair near their fireplace, and I knelt next to her and together we flipped through a photo album I brought, sharing my pictures with her. We were all enjoying time together until Grandma and Grandpa William had to leave because it was getting late. What a great way to start our Christmas!

The next morning around 10:00 am, we received an unexpected call from Grandpa. With a wavering voice, he told us that Grandma Gail had passed away. They had gotten up in the morning as usual. He got dressed and left to attend a men's Bible study. When he returned, she was lying on the bed, as though she had just fallen backward, and appeared asleep. We had just spent the day with her yesterday! My uncle Dave was already on his way to the airport to return home when he got the call about Grandma. He and his wife immediately returned to Bob's and Grace's house. With heavy hearts that certainly weren't prepared for this, we all gathered for the next few days, sharing memories, crying, worrying about Grandpa, and preparing for the funeral. Drew and I were able to stay a few extra days to spend a little more time with the whole family and attend Grandma's funeral.

A few days after Grandma Gail's passing, I got a call from my mom in Minnesota, informing me that Grandma Elle had died too. Sadly, we were not able to attend her funeral. We had been gone too long from our jobs and Drew couldn't miss any more work. The greatest part of this story for me is that Karli was able to meet both of her great-grandmothers within days of each other before they died. *What a miracle!* Still, that was an extremely difficult Christmas. The following year, Aunt Grace presented each family with a gift. This special handmade gift was a stuffed bear that was dressed in Grandma Gail's clothing, and each bear wore her costume jewelry. The bear I received was wearing that dark purple suit, the one that she wore when we got our picture taken together on Christmas Day. My bear, Gail Bear, sits in a tiny doll-sized rocking chair in our guest room as a reminder of how special family is, and of how our Lord works all things together.

Out of the blue, I began to experience the same horrific cramping again. It was debilitating, to the point of being doubled over in agony. After it went on for a couple of days, I realized I might be pregnant again. My breasts were very tender, too. Instead of taking a pregnancy test, we went back to our same doctor. He ordered another urine test, but this time we didn't have to wait for the results. He confirmed that I was indeed pregnant again. These cramps, however, were worse than before, triggering the possibility of another problem. He concluded that I had an ectopic pregnancy. An ectopic pregnancy, in this case a tubal pregnancy, is when the fertilized egg gets caught or stuck in the fallopian tube. It cannot remain there. Either the fallopian tube will burst or the egg will die. This news was very scary for us! All I knew is that it hurt so badly, but I didn't want to lose a baby. Now remembering the pain from my first pregnancy, it began to make sense. Karli must have started out as an ectopic pregnancy but she somehow "miraculously" was moved through my fallopian tube to my uterus, where she became implanted and grew to be a healthy baby! *WOW*. This realization was so much to take in. But for this little life, there was little hope. Since I wasn't very far along, the doctor determined that I needed an injection that would stop cell growth and dissolve the tissue, thus terminating our baby's life. We were heartbroken. Perhaps this one too could have eventually made its way to my uterus, but with such pain already, my life was in danger. To live with this knowledge of that tiny life being gone, but knowing that it WAS a life, gives me hope of one day meeting this child of ours in heaven.

I took on a new job in a new career path several months after Karli was born. This time I went to work for a home remodeling company that also had a natural stone fabrication shop. This was the company that had done some remodeling and added a master suite to our home, and since we felt comfortable with the owner, he offered me a position as the scheduler at their fabrication shop, Architectural Granite and Marble. I knew absolutely nothing about natural stone and how to get the measurements for installations, but I learned it. I like the whole remodeling process, so it came easily to me. Plus, I enjoy working with people, so selling a product that they already wanted was simple. Sadly, the economy took a downward turn, and with so many other fabricators trying to undercut the pricing, they had to let me go after two years. I immediately went to work for one of the suppliers of our granite and marble slabs and ran their warehouse and sales. I enjoyed this job too. Granite and marble slabs are a beautiful all-natural product, displaying the longevity of time and how something that has been under such intense pressure can become something so strong!

When I learned that I was pregnant for the third time, I was scared. Not because of motherhood, but because I was afraid my boss would let me go if he knew I was pregnant. It took me four months to tell him. He calmly told me not to worry, and that I would always have a job there if I wanted one. I was reassured with those same words for five months. So, I planned on taking a three-month maternity leave-of-absence, and he said again, "Not to worry."

The great news is that during this entire pregnancy, I did NOT experience the awful cramping! I had the same aversions to garlic and mayonnaise, yet no cravings. The only difficulty I encountered was during labor. The epidural I was given only partially worked. It numbed about a third of me, mainly the right side, but not the left. The nurse gave me a second epidural, and this one helped a little more, but I still felt about fifty percent of those labor pains. They were excruciating! But, I would go through it all over again to have this remarkable child!

Dane Jennings Wiseman arrived May 12, 2005. Now we had one boy and one girl! Our little family finally felt complete.

During my maternity leave, I checked in weekly with my boss to see how work was handling my absence. The fourth week I was out, I called as usual, and he said sorry, but he had to replace me. They couldn't hold the position for me because the job wasn't getting done with me being away. If I wanted a job after my maternity leave, then I would have to see if there were any openings. *Ugh.* So the "not to worry" wasn't meant for me, but rather for his peace of mind. He never intended to allow me to have my three months' leave and didn't have the decency to tell me that. After a short battle, I was able to collect unemployment for six months. *That minimal income wouldn't last long, and then what?*

Drew had been at his Pearl Drums job for sixteen years now, and was as close to the top of that ladder as he would ever be. It just wasn't enough to support us as a sole income. So, time for a change. That probably meant moving.

While at Pearl Drums, Drew had taken on the role of Project Manager of a computer software implementation. He had been doing this simultaneously while also serving as Operations Manager. The relationship he built with the software company led to an employment opportunity with them. The problem was that they were based in Atlanta, Georgia. That would mean moving away from all of our friends and Drew's family. They were our sole support system. His parents had relocated from Florida to Nashville since all of their kids were living there now. If Drew took this job, we'd have to leave all of that. We had lived in the Nashville area for sixteen years, but after much prayer and new financial struggles, we decided it was the right time to go and the right job for us.

We had to get our ranch house ready to sell! It had been ours for nine years and still needed some updating, at least enough to make it look somewhat more presentable to a potential buyer. Naturally, we called on the handiest man we knew, my birth father Russell. He had come to visit us regularly since our first meeting, and he was ready to help whenever he could. He drove down from Minneapolis with his tools and got our house ready to sell. It sold in only one week and we made a nice profit.

Russell and Drew went ahead of the kids and me to our new home in the northern Atlanta area of Marietta. They spent two weeks prepping our new contemporary, cedar-sided

with wood floors and new carpet and began remodel-
ıe master bath. It was on Dane's first birthday in May of
/6 that the kids and I drove down with Drew and moved
in. What a way to celebrate! This was a new life, a new location, and hopefully some new friends. Russell stayed with us
in Marietta for six weeks, helping get us settled in and com-
pleting the renovations. Unfortunately, while he was with us,
he received a call from his brother telling him that his mother, my paternal grandmother, Fern Walker, had passed away.
This was hard news for Russell to accept since he had been
away from his family for so many weeks. He finished up what
he could and left the next day with a long drive back home for
his mother's funeral.

Russell, who to me is my "father," has become an integral part
of our family. The kids absolutely adore him, mostly because
he spends time with them. He plays games with them, chases
them, reads with them, takes them to movies, and gives fully
of himself to them. He comes down at least once every year to
visit us if he can. For a man who hasn't ever raised children of
his own, he does a great job of being a grandfather. His handy
carpentry and home repair skills have allowed us to remodel
a kitchen, move a laundry room to the basement, and lay tile
in various areas. He built a massive deck for us with a radius
edge which was a show stopper when we sold that house. In
spite of all this, it took me a long time to fully accept him. I
don't know if it was because of my dad, or what, but it took me
fifteen years to tell Russell that I loved him. I know he deeply
longed to hear it for years, since he regularly stated that he
loved me, but I just wasn't ready. When I did finally tell him,
he completely believed it and wept with joy.

Drew and I found a church home in Marietta. It took us several months to agree on one. We both wanted a Bible-believing and teaching church, and he also wanted some incredible music. The irony that we could even agree on one is because I was raised Lutheran, he was raised Episcopalian, we had attended a Presbyterian church for fifteen years, and then we decided to attend a Baptist church! We have learned that it doesn't matter the denomination as long as the Church is teaching from God's Word, proclaiming the Gospel of our Lord Jesus as Savior, and helping to carry out the mission of sharing His story of love to the ends of the earth. This very large church, Johnson Ferry Baptist, did just that. I realized that I had not been baptized since I personally accepted the Lord way back when I was thirteen, so on October 31, 2010, I was publicly baptized in front of 1,000 people at our church and was given the opportunity to share my two-minute videotaped testimony with those in attendance that morning. During my testimony, I explained how I have been adopted three times: the first two times by different families and the third time by my Heavenly Father into His family. Six months after my testimony in church, a young girl saw us eating out at Wendy's, and she asked me if I was the one who had been adopted two times and had shared my story in church. She had been touched by my testimony and remembered it!

Meanwhile, we experienced changes within the Wiseman clan. Thanksgiving 2008 proved to be a difficult one when Drew's father's prostate cancer came back with a vengeance. Donald had been dealing with it for more than fifteen years. The severity of it this time caused an extended hospital stay, then he was moved home for his last few weeks and was taken care of by his wife, Janet. She was by his side every minute possible, talking to him, helping him in every way, and keeping him comfortable. What a testimony it was to all of us to see such devoted love after forty-seven years of marriage! As the family watched his life slowly fade, there was no denying the full life he had lived. He had been a chaplain's assistant in World War II, had a Master's Degree in music, owned a travel agency in Florida, started an Episcopal church in Frankfurt, Germany, and was an Episcopal priest for more than fifty years. Donald passed away peacefully just a few days before Christmas. His legacy lives on through his wife and four children and the thousands of lives he influenced and touched.

When our son Dane was about three years old, I began to have these terrible dreams about him dying. He would either drown, fall over a balcony, or slip into a huge sinkhole. During the course of about a year and a half, I had *seven* of these dreams. It was traumatizing! Perhaps it was the result of an incident that occurred that summer.

Dane and Karli were playing in our backyard on the white cedar playground that we had bought and set up for them the summer before. This was the mack daddy of playgrounds! We created a large level area in the yard with landscaping timbers around it and filled it with mulch. There were two swings nestled in between two towers. The bigger second story play area on the left side was covered, with a slide on the front side and a cargo net on the back. To the right of the swings, was another tower, this one was uncovered. There was a ramp to climb up in the front, and on the backside of the structure, there was a knotted rope for climbing straight up or down next to a fireman's pole.

The beauty was I could watch them from my eight-foot-wide kitchen window as I prepared the meals or cleaned up, which is what I was doing when it happened. I heard this noise. I thought it was crying, but not any type of crying I had heard from Dane before. It was more strained, raspier. I looked up and saw him slowly stumbling towards me from the playground, while he held his neck. I instantly knew something was wrong, so I ran out back to meet him, wondering what the heck had happened. As I approached him, I could hear him quietly crying, but noticed his neck had a purple line on it. I hugged him asking if he was OK and what had happened. He couldn't talk, only gasp. That's when I saw it. He had a one inch, dark purple ring around eighty percent of his neck. He had nearly hung himself! I was horrified as the realization of what he just went through coursed through me. *How scary that must have been for him!* Karli came over asking what was wrong. She didn't even know this had happened! She was playing in the covered tower and didn't see anything. Apparently, he was up on the smaller tower and about to go down the rope. He had innocently looped the rope around his neck, and jumped. He hung there for a second . . . when somehow he miraculously was freed. The more I pictured this, the harder it was for me to control my emotions. Dane had been hanging there helplessly by a rope in my yard without any of us noticing it, except for the Lord. *Thank you, God, for knowing and seeing my son!* Dane was spared that day, and I will never stop thanking God for that. I also didn't let Dane use that rope for about another year. It was off limits to everyone. *Why did I leave it there?* As a reminder to all of us of what the Lord did that day.

Around this time, I had made significant progress in writing my life story, but then I struggled with how to proceed. Not sure of the legal ramifications of telling this with some of the individuals involved, and not having permission to use their names, I couldn't decide if I should risk publishing this book using their rightful names, or if I should use an alias for everyone as well as change the names of the cities mentioned. I considered writing under a pen name to avoid the risk of getting sued, especially by my dad or his family, for defamation of character or libel reasons. Essentially it could come down to his word against mine. I suppose I *could* have waited until he passed away, but there would be his family left behind who might frown upon me sharing this and take action accordingly! My dilemma was if I were to write it under an assumed pen name, then I could never share my testimony publicly or give an interview about my life. If I used real names, there would always be that risk of hurting someone or embarrassing them. I didn't want that for my family or for anyone else! So, this story in written form was shelved for a couple of years.

During this time, I continued to sense the need to "do something" with it. My decision came in the form of a prayer: "Lord, you have given me this life, and this is your story, not mine. If you want this book to reach many, then you need to work this out. Please direct me with what to do next, and how to proceed. I give it to you. I trust you with it. If this is to remain just a biography for my children, then here it is. If this is to be for others to learn from and help them find peace in forgiveness and trusting in your divine plan, then you need to make it happen. I will wait for you."

nods of approval

Our little dog Crystal, a Border Collie mix, loved to take walks with me every day. We would walk anywhere from one to five miles. During this time together, I would often find myself "thinking on these things." I would read the Bible on my iPhone, look up other's interpretations of scripture, and dwell on one or two topics at a time. A few weeks prior, I had helped a friend of mine proofread his book which he had just finished writing for families with children, and it dealt with the topics of dating, talking to your kids about sex, etc. While walking one day shortly after having proofread his book, it got me thinking about my own shelved book. So, I began to pray about it *again*. Immediately the Holy Spirit gave me the answer, and it floored me. The thought had NEVER crossed my mind to actually talk to dad about his opinion of it, or to get his feelings on the matter! We hadn't had much communication with each other since our visit in Nashville, some thirteen years ago! Sure there had been a couple of "Happy Birthday" or "Happy Father's Day" emails and cards, but nothing any deeper than that, nothing of any significance. Now to consider this most direct and honest route filled me with great excitement, and anticipation. This was His answer! I rushed to get back home with a renewed sense of urgency, much to Crystal's dismay (she wasn't ready to go back home yet). As soon as I got home, I quickly emailed my brother to get Dad's email address, and he sent it to me the same day.

Here in the Atlanta area, we experienced two rounds of severe weather, which was national news. Of course, most of the country was experiencing the snow, ice and poor conditions at the same time. Schools were closed for several days, which meant children playing in the snow, drying wet mittens and gloves, making many cups of hot chocolate, watching movies, playing a variety of board games and card games, and attempting to control electronics time for both of our kids. I wouldn't trade those days for anything, but it did not allow me to take a couple of hours to write a heartfelt and critical email to my dad. Apparently, my brother had mentioned to him that I had asked for his email address, and it must have come as great news to dad because he emailed me three times in a matter of four days, wondering when was I going to email him, had I emailed him, and informing me of his best email address. The kids finally went back to school, and on that Wednesday, I sat down and wrote my dad an email, telling him the things that one would tell a really good friend that they hadn't seen in many years, such as describing each child and both of their activities, telling of Drew and his work and his passion for playing and writing music, sharing about our church and our involvement there, including how being a part of the Prayer Ministry had impacted my life and increased my faith, and finally giving him the details of how I have been agonizing and struggling with the writing and publishing of my life's story, especially the part that involved him and incest. I wrote earnestly. I wrote from my heart. Then I waited.

Our daughter Karli was in the Middle School Choir at our church, and they had practice on Wednesday evenings. Since Drew had to work, I typically took her and dropped her off, and then I would walk the indoor track in our church gymnasium, sometimes alone but most often with a friend. This particular evening, one of my dearest friends, Melissa, walked with me. We shared details about our week, the ups and downs, and I told her of my decision to email dad and briefed her on what it said. After an hour of walking, we sat down. The thought to check my email crossed my mind, so I did. At the top of my downloads, I saw an email from my dad. *Whoa! He sure replied fast*! It had only been about six hours since I sent him that email, and I figured he would need time to digest the news, talk to his wife, and decide what to do! Nervously, I reread to Melissa the portion of the email I had written to him that dealt with the book. Then, I read out loud to her, his email back to me: "Thank you for the email. I would like to talk with you by phone, at a time that is convenient for you. I am all for you writing your story . . . I want to assure you I am all for you in writing your story. I would like to talk by phone since we can't sit face to face and talk. Hope to hear from you . . ."

I had to stop reading. The tears just starting flowing! Melissa reached over and hugged me, and I was, simply put, AMAZED at how God had chosen to work. This meant that the book could go forward! The details of how did not matter yet at this time. My dad had expressed a desire for us to talk, and a desire for this to be told! That was a true miracle. He had shared other details about his family, his wife, his grand-children, their faith, and how he so desired for the grandkids to know and trust in Jesus! *Wow.* I hadn't even considered what the Lord might be doing in his life. *Why hadn't I thought about that? Why hadn't I prayed for him?* He is just as equally a child of God as much as I am, yet I had failed to consider that.

Dad and I set a time to call and talk on the phone. This was huge! It put me in motion to call my Grandfather William, my mom, my sister-in-law, a fellow prayer warrior, and my hus-band and ask them all to take time and pray about this: that my attitude be one of peace and gentleness, and that dad and I could experience some healing in our time of sharing, and that God be glorified in this.

On the Friday I was supposed to call my dad, I was at peace, and surprisingly calm. Sure, I didn't know exactly what I would say, but I had confidence that it would all be OK. I just needed to be honest, share, and be loving. What else are we asked to do? To love others is the greatest command! It's funny how I felt such a strong love for my dad now, not even knowing what he might say. It didn't matter. This whole situ-ation was still in God's hands. He had a plan.

I called my dad at 12:30 pm Eastern time, and he answered im-mediately. Our first few minutes we made small talk about the unusual weather we all were having to deal with. He told me how his health had been for several years and how his heart and back surgeries, along with Fibromyalgia, caused him to need many pills, at one point taking eighty pills a day, which naturally began to affect his memory. His wife found a more natural, healthy way for them to eat and live, which began to help his health and weight, but didn't appear to bring back any of those lost memories. His wife had left the prior day to be with their daughter, his stepdaughter, who was about to have their grandchild, but the snowstorm was causing chaos with power outages and huge drifts of snow, which made traveling to the hospital extremely difficult for her. He thought perhaps my call was his wife informing him of the baby's status. He must have looked at the clock to check the time because he quickly changed the topic to the purpose of our phone call.

What did I want to talk about? What were my concerns? What did I need to know? His voice sounded a little smaller, a little weaker, and his northern Yankee accent was more apparent. It was so refreshing to be speaking with him! I didn't feel any hurt, anger or tension. He sounded as though he was being totally transparent, and honest, with his heart and life open and exposed. Then my book came up. Dad knew that I wanted to publish it, but since he hadn't read it, would doing so cause him to change his mind? We agreed that I would send him the first two chapters, which dealt with me while I was a child and when he was a major part of my life's story. Even though he hadn't read it yet, he still insisted that I go ahead and tell it! It was agreed that it would be best to use an alias for him (and his family) so as not to bring any shame or uneasiness upon them now or in the future, should any of their extended family or friends hear about it or read it. I thought this was a fair way to proceed. With that, we said our goodbyes. Our conversation had lasted 35 minutes.

WOW. My heart was overjoyed, overflowing with gratitude and truly humbled by the way the Lord had worked this out. I sat back, letting more tears flow, and worshipped the Lord.

My first call, after speaking with Drew and updating him, was to my mom. She had been anticipating the news of how it had gone. Mom was genuinely happy but seemed somewhat bewildered at this turn of events! We spoke about it at length, with her summary of it being this: "It's amazing to see how the Lord can take such sinful people, who shared in such a painful story by way of our hurtful actions and words and weave it into a tale of sweet forgiveness, with each one of us having been transformed and willing to go forward with this. Knowing that we all have been forgiven, by God, by each other, and by our own selves, just goes to show that the Lord has written a happy ending!"

Even though dad didn't recall any of those events from so many years ago, it didn't matter because he had been set free of them. The hurts between mom and I had been released and set free. The act of forgiveness is necessary for all people involved because, without it, we all suffer the pain of memory. If we let it go, as the Lord does for us, then it is gone. It is GONE.

Later that day, I emailed dad the first two chapters as promised. He must have read them immediately because I got his reply just a few hours later. He said, "There is so much in there I don't remember. If that's what you remember, that is how you need to write it so you can finish your book. Yes, I would like to read it, so sending it the way this came, works. Thank you. Love you." He was willing to let this be told, to be shared! No doubt the Lord had been working with him too. To read of his past had to be painful for him, but to be willing to allow it to become public, had to be something truly of the Almighty One.

With so much approval, it was time to move forward with this story, but I didn't know who to get to help me. I thought Hazel, the amazing mother of a good friend of mine and whose family I had also lived with in Kansas City for a time, could be the one. In doing research, I found her on Facebook, and we got reacquainted. Hazel had been like a mom to me, treating me like she would her own daughter, accepting me for my faults, and allowing me to be in their home. Her editing history with a big publishing company would certainly be valuable if she was willing to consider helping me. I got up the nerve to ask her if she would read my manuscript, and give me any advice or critiquing necessary to help me finish this book. She agreed! And yes, I was given advice, positive reinforcement, and constructive criticism that made me pause enough to question whether or not I could truly complete writing this story. I began to doubt my ability. Writing is not my strength. Yet I just knew that there was a remarkable story here to be told and shared with others—a story that some may be able to relate to and find a common thread in their lives, ultimately encouraging them to continue on their journey to healing and happiness. I had to entrust this process to the Lord.

Our lives took a turn which once again resulted in shelving this story during a season of change.

let go and go

Johnson Ferry Baptist Church (JFBC) had been our church home for nearly ten years. The children grew up in it! Our world revolved around church services, Sunday school, choir, Upward sports like soccer, basketball, baseball and flag football, mission trips for Karli, and youth group outings for Dane, Wednesday night dinners, and especially our many good friends.

Drew and I both volunteered on Sundays during the worship service. He occasionally played keyboards in the contemporary service, and I was a camera operator two Sundays a month for the contemporary service. I felt led to be a part of the Prayer Ministry and even helped lead a women's Bible study. When I was looking for a part-time job, I looked into what JFBC had open so that I could earn some income while still serving within our church, but nothing was working out. When my grandfather William had come to visit us when he was ninety-two, I set up a quick meeting for him with our pastor, Bryant Wright, since he had been the president of the Southern Baptist Convention for two years, and Grandpa had been a Baptist pastor for more than sixty years! You would think that seeing me would be Grandpa's highlight of that trip, but nope, it was meeting our pastor.

Meanwhile, Drew had been working for Manhattan Associates in Atlanta for nine years and was ready to make a change in his career path. He had a friend who was also a former boss at Manhattan Associates who had begun working in a high position at Intelligrated, another computer software company in Alpharetta, Georgia. He thought Drew would be a great asset to his team and encouraged him to consider making a career move. As Drew contemplated this, he knew there would be some negative ramifications, and perhaps, even some legal issues involved in leaving his present employer. He had signed a contract when he became employed at Manhattan, along with other binding agreements, and we didn't want him to burn any bridges or cause any financial problems by maybe getting sued or worse because of these contracts. We decided the best plan was to pray about his potential new job. Pray we did! Drew decided to pursue this new venture, and his employer fought back. They didn't want to lose him, not after so many years, and especially not to another software company. So, out came the legal papers. Drew and I kept praying about it. If this move was of the Lord, then He would have to fight these battles. Our hands were tied. The non-compete clause that he had to sign every year was causing some difficulty. It stated that he could not work for any competitor on their published list in doing the same or similar job capacity that he had held within the last two years. Now their lawyers were getting involved. As Drew and I kept praying about this, we witnessed many miracles. The title and job description for Drew's most recent position had changed, which meant his latest role at Manhattan, which had changed two years prior, was not the same position he would have at Intelligrated, making his non-compete clause null and void. If he hadn't changed roles within the last two years, he wouldn't have been able to quit and accept a new job at Intelligrated. But, this was all in God's timing, He had already worked it out! This was just one of many little signs along the way that proved to us the Lord was with us in this new endeavor. What a way to encourage someone's faith, by witnessing how the Lord works in His time for our good. Manhattan didn't offer any blessings but they reluctantly agreed to let Drew go to their competitor. They were no match for our Lord.

Once Drew had been at Intelligrated for about a year, we considered moving to a nicer house in a better neighborhood setting to be closer to his new job. This move would likely require changing schools, possibly even school districts, but that was OK since both kids were graduating to new schools anyway, with Karli moving into high school and Dane moving into middle school. If we were going to move, this was the time and year to do it, during the summer.

We began getting our house ready to sell. With so many upgrades and remodeling already completed, there wasn't that much to do. We asked for the highest price ever in our tiny neighborhood, and in just a couple of weeks, we got it.

The hunt for a new house began in earnest since the clock was ticking! Up until now, we had been looking online, going to open houses and even had some viewings with our realtor, but nothing felt just right. We wanted a home in a great school district, with a big yard, at least 3,000 square feet, five bedrooms and three baths, an office, a high ceiling, and a great play space for the kids. It also had to have a two-car garage with extra storage. We preferred it to be a ranch house, but those were harder to come by. If it needed remodeling, even better. We had done that a few times by now, so putting our own stamp on our new house was fine by us. But as we looked and looked, nothing was quite right. We didn't see anything that was worth giving up what we already had. We didn't want to leave our church so that limited our search criteria. We looked within a forty-minute radius, and there was NOTHING. As we were running out of time before we had to choose to stay or rent a place and store our stuff, I sat down to pray. I was the one who wasn't willing to give up our church. Drew had mentioned several times about moving further away, perhaps even far enough out that we couldn't go to JFBC, and I had been adamant and said, "NO!" every time. Now, seeing how critical the timing was, and recognizing that I had been putting our church on a pedestal and wasn't willing to go where ever the Lord led us, even if that meant to another church family, I broke down and offered up our future to Him, completely. I said, "Lord, if you want us to move out and to another city, and be a part of a different church, then so be it. I can't keep fighting you. I give my family, our home, our church, and our lives back to you. I am sorry. We will go where you would have us to go." It's funny how when you're willing, He will take you up on it! A couple of days later, we saw a house online in Cumming, Georgia—an hour away, in a different city and county, out in the country—that looked like it could be home.

After visiting this house in a stunning neighborhood where we felt very out of place, we found a different home in that same neighborhood that fit everything on our checklist, and made an offer within a week. Long story short, it's ours! Now we just had to find a temporary place to live for two weeks between moving out and moving in. We rented a "cabin" (that's a generous term) on Lake Lanier, which was unfortunate for us because it was over the 4th of July and the cost was about $3,000 for two weeks. Mind you it had a dock, but that was the ONLY saving grace for this shoddy, bug-infested, poison ivy-riddled, moldy, overgrown, tiny cottage. When I say bug infested, imagine ten dead cockroaches on the floor, about fifty dead bugs on the stove, spider webs on the steps and dining room table, and that's just the bugs! Needless to say, we were so thrilled when our two weeks were up, and we moved into our new home!

The next challenge we faced was finding our new church home. *How could any church compare to JFBC?* It had so much to offer everyone of any age. *What could be out here in the country?* We had heard about Browns Bridge Church, a sister church of televangelist Andy Stanley's North Point Community Church. We knew one of their worship leaders, who used to attend JFBC and moved to Browns Bridge Church. We visited there a couple of times, and although we really enjoyed the teaching, the setting, and the worship music, it just didn't feel right, not like our new church home. The kids loved it but Drew and I were doubtful.

The next week we decided to try a smaller contemporary-looking, non-denominational church called Mountain Lake, and it was even a little closer to our home. The name meant a lot to me since that's my kind of dream-home setting—a mountain lake home. *Yeah, I said that.* I tried the church because of the name. When we walked in the front door, we were kindly greeted, and I immediately felt at home, taking in the large windows and the gathering of many people in the foyer drinking coffee and fellowshipping. I felt a little nudge from the Holy Spirit. The atmosphere was so peaceful and comfortable. We strolled around for a few minutes, trying to get the layout, found the entrance to the sanctuary, and walked in. Seating was stadium-like, with a stage up front and screens on the side walls, and I saw two cameras with volunteers waiting for the service to begin. Oooh! Now I really felt good about this. My first thought was, *"Hey, maybe one day I can help by being a camera operator here."* The worship music was spot-on, the new pastor's message was sound biblical teaching for the common man, and I was sold. Drew took a little more time to come around, and the kids even longer, but Mountain Lake Church became our new church family. I had to be willing to let go of JFBC so we could become a part of Mountain Lake. I learned from this that we are all a part of the Church family. The question is: are we willing to go when He leads us somewhere different?

family travel

Our family had been happily living "up-in-Cumming" for one year. The summer of 2017—just before our 25th wedding anniversary—Drew and I decided to make our anniversary celebration a family affair by taking a two-week vacation out west. We flew from Atlanta, Georgia, to Portland, Oregon, where we spent the 4th of July week with my birth mother's family, the Davises. Grandpa William had just turned ninety-five, so it was a special gift for me to be able to spend some quality time with him, not knowing how much longer he would be with us. Hanging out with my aunt and uncle and several cousins while celebrating our country's Independence Day with them, and sitting out on their massive back deck overlooking their forty acres, while everyone told their best stories and teased each of the cousins, made for never a dull moment. Picking fresh cherries, playing yard games, exploring the old barn, sitting in the hot tub at night, and especially going to Haystack Rock at Cannon Beach, were all fabulous memories for us, especially for the kids. On Sunday, Grandpa wanted the four of us to join him at his church and asked me to sit next to him. He couldn't see well, hear well or walk well, but he was there, and I was next to him. I cherished that time! The day before we left, I said, "Goodbye" to Grandpa, knowing that I likely wouldn't see him again in this life. I must have cried for an hour afterward. This man meant so much to me! His humor, which not everyone always appreciated, would always make me laugh. His jokes, his smile, his foot rubs, his deeply rooted faith and his desire to share the Lord with anyone at any time, all made for truly a remarkable man, and someone whom I will always hold extremely close to my heart.

We spent two days in Seattle, Washington, then flew out to California, where we spent three days in San Francisco and then headed to Los Angeles. From there we rented a car and drove out to the Sequoia National Forest for two days, then went back to L.A., where we rented a house right on the beachfront. For the kids, this whirlwind two-week trip was filled with experiences they will hopefully never forget, especially since I took literally 1,600 pictures to remind them of it!

We had been home for a couple of days when the kids went to a week-long church retreat for teenagers in Florida. So with some time on my hands, I flew to Minnesota to see more of my family, both the ones who adopted me and Russell, my birth father. It had been thirteen years since I had been up north . . . it was time.

Russell greeted me at the airport. It had been a year since I saw his kind face. His gentle spirit was reflected in his long, tender hug. He was so happy I was coming to spend time with him! We had three days together during that trip, though not consecutively, and he wanted to make the most of it. We ate lunch at Ikea, and he took me to the Mall of America which was only about ten minutes from his apartment. Walking around with him on every floor and taking silly pictures at LegoLand sums up how much fun we had together. He is a good companion. Later we drove to his apartment, which he rented from an older lady who really enjoyed his company as well as his handyman skills. She gave me accommodations in her spare bedroom, and we shared her bathroom. Russell had the whole basement to himself. He had remodeled it and created a nice apartment space with a full kitchen, full bath, laundry area, bedroom, and sitting area. It was quite comfortable! Russell and I went out to dinner, played games, cards, ate, looked at pictures, and just enjoyed being together. It was good for both of us to have this time together.

The next day, I had arranged to drive to Wisconsin and visit Peniel's Pastor Ken and Mrs. Melodee. Peniel had closed down a few years ago since there wasn't anyone else willing or able to continue that ministry. Both Pastor Ken and Mrs. Melodee were getting older and couldn't manage such an undertaking anymore. But, they were still living in the same town in a tiny apartment. I couldn't wait to see them! We had kept in touch via Facebook, but that wasn't the same as hugging them and talking face-to-face.

I found their room number and knocked. Mrs. Melodee opened the door, and she looked just as I remembered, only her hair was grayer. We hugged tightly, and I didn't want to let go. This woman had been like a mother to me for five years of my life, during my critical teenage years and even afterward. She had taught me, encouraged me, spanked me, counseled me, loved me and led me by example on how to live a Christian life that serves and loves others. It was so good to see her! She led me inside their apartment, and there was Pastor Ken. He was seated in his big chair with a walker by his side, his hair white as snow, and his smile stretching from ear to ear. I walked over to him and hugged him as he remained seated. It was difficult for him to get up due to his health, but he remembered me! His dementia wasn't bad that day, and the three of us enjoyed reminiscing that morning about the glory days of Peniel. We went to Subway for lunch, but Mrs. Melodee wanted to drive us there. She was Pastor Ken's caretaker, so she helped him literally every step of the way. Her love for this man was so apparent in everything she did for him. He couldn't physically do a lot for himself, so she did it all for him, without complaint. I witnessed a great example of true love that day. I never heard her utter one harsh word or one deep sigh of frustration, or show any sign of impatience. She truly enjoyed taking care of him. They had a beautiful, long-lasting partnership that had withstood the test of time and the demands of a ministry serving thousands of troubled kids over four decades. "Lord," I prayed, "Please bless this couple who has served you faithfully with all their hearts for their entire married life!" What a testimony they were to me and thousands of others of fully trusting in the Lord. Sadly, I had to leave in order to beat Minneapolis traffic, which meant my time with them was much too short. But, I thanked the Lord for this sweet time together.

The next day was Friday. I got up early, climbed into my little rental car, honked "beep-beep" to Russell, and drove to western Minnesota to spend the weekend with my mom and older brother James. It had been so long since I had seen mom. Her many "situations"—health, husband, pets, pastoring, etc.— didn't allow her to come south to visit us over the years, so I had to go to her. Naturally, I was very frustrated but I knew that if I was going to see her, I had to go to her. My brother had been down south to visit us several times for vacation, but I hadn't been up his way, so this was going to be a good time for the three of us to be together, talk, and play our favorite card games like Canasta. The anticipation was almost overwhelming. During that two-and-a-half-hour drive west, I prayed, sang, and wondered what our time together would be like. *Would mom and I get along? Would it be like when we talk on the phone for two hours at a time? Would she be accepting of me? Would I see her as the mom I had always wanted and enjoyed talking with on the phone, or would hurts and disappointments arise and smother my expectations?* Before I would find out, mom's two brothers and their wives were joining me for lunch.

Perkins is an American casual dining restaurant found throughout the midwestern parts of the United States. It was here that I sat down with my uncles Martin and John and my aunts Jean and Nancy for a meal and a discussion of life events relating to our families. This time together, for me, was amazing. We talked about my childhood, mom and dad, Peniel, my kids, Drew, and life in the south. When we spoke about Peniel, I knew the pain they felt for me was real. It had deeply bothered them that I was sent away, and they never did understand why. Yes, they eventually knew about dad molesting me, but that only made the whole thing worse for them. So I tried to explain to them that although it seemed to be a bad call to place me at Peniel, that decision most likely saved my life. I told them I had forgiven mom and dad for all of the past things said or done. I wondered if they had forgiven my mom. Not so simple from their point of view. They filled me in on my cousins' lives, farming in today's world, and how they loved retirement. To sit with my uncle John who is also my godfather and fiercely loves me, and to sit with my other uncle Martin who has a heart as big as Texas, made my trip worth it. My aunts have faithfully stood by their husbands' sides and with dedication raised their kids all through a life-time of farming. These women loved me as much as my uncles did. Our 90-minute lunch was way too short, but we took some pictures of the five of us and went our separate ways. Now it was finally time to go see mom.

Mom's home was newly built sometime after she married an old high school friend. It was a second marriage for both of them, but seeing them together you would think they were back in high school and in love! Anyway, together they designed their house, decorated it, chose the landscaping, and enjoyed a good life there for many years, until he passed away. Now, she lives there alone and takes great pride in how neat and clean her home is. She has a story for each knick-knack that sits on her shelves and each piece of art that lines the walls. What I noticed when I walked around her house was that she had only a couple of family pictures set out. Her life had been so focused on her pastoral duties and parishioners, my younger brother's death, James' unmarried status, and my absence, that the less-is-more theory had come into play. Our Wiseman family annual calendar was hanging in the kitchen though, so I knew she still sees us and prays for us every day.

Our initial greeting was very warm, and we hugged for a few moments. It was so good to see mom again! She didn't look a whole lot different from when I had seen her before, except her hairstyle had changed. My hairstyle also changed as it does every year, so that's to be expected. She gave me the tour of her home and her garden, each with its own stories of how things came to be. It felt nice to be with her. It was comfortable. What was unusual about this visit is the last time we were together, my husband and Karli were there as well, and this time it was to be just the two of us until later the next day. My brother had to work and couldn't get there before noon on Saturday. Mom and I hadn't been alone for any length of time since before I moved to Kansas City! So, after discussing our dinner plans, we went out to eat at a local restaurant that my mom enjoys, and it was quite good. Our conversations ranged from my brother and his life to the management of her home, yard, and work. Then we discussed my world. I started to feel this small ache inside. I didn't know why.

The next morning, I went for a long walk around the country block, and when I got back, we decided it was yard work time. Out came the mower, the blower, the trimmer, and the neighbors. After being introduced to a few of her neighbors, we managed to get the yard in shape, and by lunchtime we were hungry. We only nibbled a bit since we knew we'd be going to dinner when my brother arrived.

James showed up later in the afternoon. He looked just as I remembered him too! My big brother gives great bear hugs, and I gladly received a tight one from him. He and mom were quickly talking details of the trip, sharing stories and playing their online computer games against each other. This is a common practice for them. They spend significant time challenging each other on Pogo or in some other virtual game room. As much as I love games, I have learned that engaging in these online games is addictive, so I have had to stop playing them. But they had each other, so they played as often as they could.

After discussing the pending severe weather, we decided that in the morning we would reevaluate whether a trip to our cabin was in the cards or not. It was only about an hour's drive, but the cabin sits down on a peninsula, and the electricity could easily go out, or trees could fall and trap us down there. Meanwhile, we spent Saturday evening playing lots and lots of cards. To watch the two of them was fun. They have this beautiful relationship between mother and son that is full of laughter and jokes. They spend every holiday and long weekends during the summer at the cabin together. This would account for their private jokes or stories that I needed them to explain to me regularly. By midnight, we were finally ready for bed.

First thing Sunday morning, they were back at the games. This was slightly annoying, as it left me out of the fun, but to be fair, I had told mom before I came that I didn't want to intrude. I just wanted to be a part of their daily lives. We had decided not to go to church with the hopes that the weather would hold out and we could make the trek to the cabin. We packed up and left by noon, each of us driving our own cars there. I would need to leave the next morning for Minneapolis, James would need to leave Tuesday morning for work, and mom, well, she had no time limit. We played follow the leader with James leading. It was quite the caravan! When we pulled into the neighborhood, I turned on my phone camera and recorded the drive down to the cabin. It didn't look much different than it had forty years ago when we would spend a week there as a family! The minimal changes made it easy to find the little house. We parked on the grassy knoll.

The beauty of this place was its quaintness. It is a 1951 bungalow on about half an acre. Lakefront property these days is in high demand so their choice to build it on a private peninsula had served to make the property value increase significantly. If you could imagine a 700-square-foot house, with two bedrooms, a living room, an eating area, and a kitchen, then that's the house. Through the years they had added an enclosed front porch and a tiny bathroom, but for the first couple of decades, the bathroom was outside in their homey and accommodating outhouse! Even as children, we were told to go outside if we needed to use the bathroom since the plumbing in this cabin was on septic and had a holding tank that was quite expensive to empty out. But the memories of this little cabin were great. The view of the lake was priceless. Due to winter erosion from ice, the beachfront was now literally about forty feet from the front door. The dock had changed over the years, from a long one to a very short one. James would keep his canoe out here for the summertime fun but lately he kept his little sailboat at home. There wasn't sufficient storage for it.

I got out of the car and strolled the lush, green, grassy lot. It didn't look that different than from when I was little. This was going to be fun. There are about thirty trees that provide shade throughout the year and plenty of leaves for raking in the fall, but the recent storms had left lots of broken limbs for James to cut up. He brought out his chainsaw and got to work. I helped mom unload the cars, then heard the lawnmower starting up, only to see James cutting the grass! *Dang, we had just gotten here, and all he wanted to do was get busy.* Mom and I finished unpacking the food in the itty bitty kitchen, and she walked me to my "room." I got the old 1960's pull-out couch. It was pretty comfortable for me because it was still hard. They don't make them any more like they used to.

After all the work was done, James and I decided to go for a canoe ride. He got out his rigged canoe with floats on both sides, and away we went. The water was calm on our side of the peninsula. We paddled down the beachfront for about a mile, then went back to go around the peninsula. At the tip near the sandbar, we encountered stronger winds and small waves but paddled hard enough to make it around to the other side. The waves continued to splash us and caused us to drift a bit, but James is a big strong guy, so he kept us at a safe distance from the rocks and docks. Many of the homes and cabins here had been updated or completely torn down with new ones built in their places. It was oddly quiet except for the water splashing on the sides of the canoe. Not many people were there this weekend. We paddled for about 45 minutes as he shared who lived where and what they had done to their places, then we returned home.

Next, it was time for some fishing. There is a good variety of fish in this lake, like sunfish, bluegill, bass, trout, and catfish. James and I set up a couple of chairs at the end of the dock, cast out, and waited. OK, my cast wasn't so great, but James's line went out pretty far. As luck would have it, I caught the first fish! My wiggly worm attracted a tiny sunfish, which I joked about having for dinner, but he laughed and said, "Nooo," and threw it back. I really enjoyed that time alone with him. It had been far too many years since we had spent time together.

Dinner was simple, as was the cleanup, so we decided to jump into game time. Mom kept joking around with James, her being silly with her big smile, and him feeding off of her spirit and the stories of neighbors or something they remembered, and the banter began. I would ask questions about their stories but didn't have a whole lot to share or add to them. I was feeling more of that ache. But, let the games begin! We played multiple rounds of Canasta, but honestly, I don't remember who won anything. I was thoroughly enjoying playing the games with them, but kind of wished for more conversation that would involve my world or a topic I could at least relate to. The sense that I was a guest rather than a family member was beginning to overtake me. Several things throughout the last twenty-four hours made me feel this way. Now, watching and hearing them, seeing their strong relationship as mother and son, and recognizing that my absence for so many years had an effect on how this was playing out, really began to bring me down. They weren't doing anything wrong. They weren't ignoring me or being rude or mean. The truth was, I was not a significant part of their lives, nor had I been for thirty-eight years, and it was playing out right now. That's just the way it was. No faults. No blame. The fact is that I was a guest, and this was fun but temporary, like a vacation, which made me realize it was just that, a vacation rather than a family reunion.

That night I went to my couch feeling sorry for myself. I couldn't define it then but I knew that this heaviness on my heart was wearing me down. I cried myself to sleep.

The next morning was Monday, and I needed to leave by 10:00 am. Well, that was my goal. We each made our own little breakfast, I packed up, and loaded up my little rental car. But, there just had to be some memorable pictures of this occasion, so James and I each got our cameras, and got busy. We all sat on this tiny, old wooden bench that creaked as we sat there. The picture I really wanted to get as a keepsake was with me in the middle and them on each side of me. My memory of the three of us. Then we all hugged goodbye, and I drove away.

To say that I cried literally for the entire first hour of that drive is no exaggeration. I even had to pull over. *Why? Why was I so sad? What had caused this engulfing sorrow? Was it something mom had said or done? Why couldn't I stop crying?* I prayed. I cried. I prayed. I kept crying. I didn't even want to listen to my music. There were no answers. It was as though the realization of what I had hoped for, wasn't there. I wasn't the daughter that mom had always wanted. I wasn't a part of her life except for an occasional phone call and the holiday cards. She and my brother had a great relationship. He had been there. I hadn't. She hadn't been down to visit us or see her grandchildren in eleven years. I had moved far away from where she was. There was no easy answer. In my heart, I eventually came to the conclusion that our relationship will always be there, but a distant one in every way, specifically physically and emotionally. But she is still my mom, and for that I am very thankful. I will always love her, and I know she loves me, no matter our circumstances or the distances that separate us.

As I was nearing the end of my trip to Minnesota, the one person left on the list to see was my dad. The last time I saw him in person was in Nashville before we had children. That visit didn't go so well. Since then, he and I had emailed, talked on the phone, and had gotten past the horrible events of our early years. Now, he was much older and his body was weaker, but his faith was far greater and his wife remained his best friend and caretaker. I had called him before my arrival in Minneapolis, and at that time, he said we would have to see if he could work it out or not. He had a doctor's visit and there was a long distance drive between where I was staying and where he lived. He could no longer drive and depended on his wife and her schedule to get him around. I so wanted to see him, to hug him, to let him know that we are OK, that the past was and had been put behind us, and the future before us had no lingering hard feelings. I only had gratitude for his decision to allow my story to be told. He called me the day we were to meet, and said he couldn't. The pain he was experiencing in his back was far too great, and he had to go back to the doctor that day to set up for surgery that absolutely had to happen. What a disappointment! To see him was to be the closure of this trip, of my family story, of that summer. I was quite sad about this, and even doubted whether or not he was being truthful with his reasons, but I had to trust that he was and that he wanted this reunion as much as I did. The surgery did happen shortly after that time, so I knew then that he had been honest with me. I only wished I could have spent a little time with him that day. *Who knows if there will be another chance?*

My mom recently retired from being a Lutheran pastor in Minnesota after twenty years in that role. I do genuinely love her and appreciate her humor in everything. She views life with the positive attitude of "why be angry when it gets you nowhere?" Rather, face it with a smile and laugh. That is the best medicine. Our past pains and hurtful memories have been forgiven, and are not dwelt on by me. Mom still tries to apologize nearly every time we speak, and tends to dwell on the, "If only I had known," but all of that past stuff cannot be dwelt on when all is forgiven! It is gone. It is done. It is finished. When you can speak of a past pain or hurtful thing and not feel any of that pain, it's now just a matter of fact . . . no emotions are involved and you know that you truly are healed.

pictures of the past

The social media giant Facebook has been my lifeline to most of my friends from across the years. I am not a big fan of writing letters or making phone calls anymore, so through Facebook I connect with a few old friends on a regular basis and many others on occasion. But there was this one guy that I had tried for many years to find, my old boyfriend David from Peniel. He was so elusive! I would scan Facebook, the phone book, and old contacts who knew him, but no one knew much about him or how to reach him. I heard that his mother had passed away several years prior, which meant he was pretty much alone with no family unless he had gotten married or had children. The likelihood of that happening was low since he had been an alcoholic for so many years and had been quite poor since what little funds he had went to alcohol and drugs rather than a phone, a computer, or even a home with an address.

One day in April, 2011, I was on Facebook and decided on a whim to try looking him up again. *Guess what!?* His name popped up! He had a brand new account, only a few days old, and only a couple of friends, so I asked to be his friend and messaged him. I waited, and nothing. Days went by and nothing. Finally, he accepted my friend request and responded to my message. The following written words from David are as he wrote them, misspellings and all. He said, "New at At facebook but learning. Had alot of struggles in life with drugs and alcohol, but am very active in AA. I'm finding both sobriety and peace with God. Use library computer so may not respond right away All for now, David P.S. My email address is . . . "

I immediately typed back, "David, OMG!! How are you doing? I heard about your mom . . . so sorry. Are you still in Buffalo/Lockport area? You have no idea how I have wondered about you and prayed for you! Thank you thank you for reaching out...when you can or want to, let me know how you are now, with the AA, etc., and your life . . . "

Three days later he replied these exact words–again, errors and all: "kari, I lived in Lockport until my mom died. That's when my life really fell apart. It took about 6 months from when she was diagnosed (lung cancer) until she died. It was the worst thing I've ever had to deal with. It went up her brain stem, and she lost her mind, she didn't even know where she was or even who I was. Hospice helped keep her at home as long as possible, but she started taking off whenever she got the chance and got violent when I tried to get her back into her apartment. She insisted she did noy live there. I can't imagine how terrifying it must have been for her, not knowing where you are and who these people are that are telling you what to do. She went into a nursing home and died about 3 weeks later. (June 2007) Watching my mom die really accelerated my drinking, not that it wasn't a problem already. I didn't know how to handle the guilt I felt about being the kind of son I was and had been, caring little about anybody else's feeling but my own. Addiction makes a person very self-centered. After I lost my job and got evicted from my apartment, I came to Niagara Falls to get out of Locport and it's bad memories and to get help with my alcohol/drug problem. I went to a 28-day program then to a halfway house for 5 months. I then went to supportive living (an apartment owned by the halfway house and supervised somewhat by there staff) I was not putting the effort required into staying sober and soon whent back to drinking. After a couple of trips to the I.C.U. at our local hospital, all alcohol related, I finally realized that unless I made some major changes, I was going to die. I had already come close more than once, so I got back into A.A. I jumped in with no reservations and followed all the suggestions they had. No one tells you what to do they only tell what worked for them. I have a sponsor who is guideing me through the 12 steps, which are our way to a new life. (look them up). It's so good to here from you! I to spent alot of time wondering where you were and how you were doing. Wher do you live, hopefully somewhere safe from the incredable wheather we are having. you have children! Are they girls or boys or both? More to say but out of time for now, God Bless, David."

The next few years there were birthday wishes sent, Christmas wishes shared, and the occasional comments on various posts between us, and each time I sensed a deep pain from him, but there were always kind words toward me.

Once he even responded to a Facebook post and said, "I believe God's love is unconditional. Sometimes it's hard to understand where God is going with things. I just trust him, no matter what I think is right (or wrong)."

Then in August 2015, he messaged me about his girlfriend of fifteen years being really quite sick, but by September, she was on the mend and getting better. He commented on how really good it felt to have good news.

In February 2016, I said, "David you are on my mind today, so I prayed for you, for strength to overcome and complete faith in His working in you. Hey, I have many pictures of you from Peniel days. I could mail them to you, but I need your address. Some are even before Peniel." I had dozens of pictures of him and thought that he needed them more than I did, hoping he would remember his youth and days at Peniel as encouragement for him to look to the faith he once professed, and seek the Lord's help in recovery.

He replied, "Thank you, Kari. It's great to be thought of and prayed for! To tell you the truth, there are a couple of issues I'm dealing with right now, so the prayers are right on time. I would LOVE the pictures! My address is . . ."

I sent them out two days later. When he received them, he thanked me profusely, reveling in memories of days long ago.

In October 2016, he messaged, "Hi Kari, I didn't mention it yesterday but, I feel like I should let you know. My girlfriend passed away in September. I haven't told a lot of people. I'm doing OK As you know, this is not the first time I've gone through this. No matter how ready you think you are when you get that call . . ."

December 1, 2017, I had an unusual dream about David. He needed to hear about it, so I messaged him, "David, I had a dream about you last night. I saw you walking away at an airport (or some other large building) with your name on the back of your jacket, and I ran up to you and HUGGED you so hard!! It was awesome to see you, if even in my dream. So, how are you doing? I believe dreams can be of the Lord and perhaps you are need of prayer or conversation about something? I am here. Let me know what I can do . . . Your friend for life, Kari."

He actually responded the same day and said, "Your pretty amazing Kari! I remeber Peniel and Onarga and driving the van. Anytime I was with you made me feel important. Your dream idea is right on. I just got out of the hospital yesterday. Old behavior can catch up with you anytime. If you would pray for me, it would mean alot. your friend for life, David."

The next day, I read his reply and responded, "David, I wept when I saw this and prayed for you immediately. The only reason that God put you on my heart–in my dream–is because He loves YOU. Don't forget that! Even if you stumble, fall, slide backward, He is still there for you to pick you up, to encourage you, loving you through it. This isn't about me or my dream, but rather about you and the Lord. Put your trust in Him to help you, thank Him when he does, and keep your focus on Him, not the things that can easily distract you. You are not alone. I will continue to pray for you, David. Perhaps in my dream, it wasn't an airport you were coming out of, but rather the hospital. I only saw you leaving a big building. Crazy how God gets so personal with us!"

David saw my message on December 3rd, 2017. No reply. I kept waiting. Still no reply.

Three months later, Drew and I were in bed getting ready to turn off the lights. Suddenly I received a message from an unknown person. It was 11:00 pm. Now I don't normally receive texts or calls so late, and when I do, I ignore them assuming it's a mistake or a relative forgetting the time difference between states. This night, I checked it. It read, *"Hello. We are sorry to bother you. We were wondering if you knew anyone in David McGarl's family. Me and my husband found your address on an envelope in his house."* I felt instant shock, bewilderment, then immediate concern, and a thousand questions ran through my head.

I replied, *"I do know David. I haven't heard from him in a few months. How do you know him? Why were you in his place long enough to find my envelope?"* They had found the envelope that still contained the pictures that I had mailed to him over a year ago. It had my name and address on it. She had been looking on David's Facebook page for friends of his, saw my name on some posts and then scoured his place for any further information about reaching me.

She begged for me to call her because it was important. Even though it was very late, I chose to call this stranger who somehow knew David. When she answered, her voice was tired, and she sounded like she had been crying, or at least stressed out. She told me her story of how they had been neighbors for a couple of years, how her young daughter adored him and called him Uncle, and how he was like a family member to them all. Then, the truth of his illness came gushing out. They had found him in his apartment with blood splattered everywhere from him coughing it up, liquor bottles everywhere, urine on the floor, mold and garbage, and David sitting in a chair, nearly dead. He was immediately taken to the nearest hospital. This kind neighbor was desperate to find someone who knew him who could help find a family member or someone who would know what to do for him. She hoped I was that person. David had told them he didn't have anyone since the death of his girlfriend over a year and a half ago, and that was why he loved being around them. It gave him the sense of belonging, being part of a family. We spoke for about 30 minutes, and I asked if we could talk the next day again to get an update, and she quickly agreed.

As soon as I put down the phone, I began praying for him and decided to get other friends of his to join me. I typed up an email to Pastor Ken and Mrs. Melodee and told them of the gravity of David's situation.

Next, I wrote an urgent post on Facebook, asking for prayers for him:

"My prayer warrior friends: I have a dear friend who is in critical condition and at death's door. He has basically given up on life and allowed his drinking to consume him resulting in a lengthy hospital stay due to cirrhosis of the liver. He's not eating and wants to die. He is a believer but has hit rock bottom. Please, please pray for him!"

162 • KARI E. WISEMAN

Then I posted the same one directly to Peniel's page, except adding that this was about David. By now, I was exhausted both physically and emotionally, so I fell asleep.

The next morning, I awoke to a flurry of questions and comments from our friends who remembered David from Peniel days. He was well liked by all who knew him. To hear of him spiraling so badly into such a state of despair was heartbreaking for us, but we were familiar with his history of drugs and alcohol, so it wasn't a huge surprise. My heart hurt so much for him! I have been depressed before but couldn't relate to his mindset (at this age) of wanting to end his life. He must have been very, very low.

Two days later, I got an update on David's condition. He was still alive, but had a partial stroke, and was diagnosed with severe cirrhosis of the liver. The doctors were familiar with David as he had been admitted multiple times before. This time, his body was shutting down and dying. The doctors gave him just a short time to live. David had given up hope and wanted to die by drinking himself to death. He even admitted this! He no longer had a mom, a dad, a girlfriend, or a job, so what was the purpose of living he thought? He spent about $4,000 in two months on alcohol. He had nothing left to live for, so why not just drink himself into oblivion? It almost worked this time. I called the hospital to see if I could talk to him directly, but he was so drugged up, he was asleep most of the time now. I asked one of the nurses to give him a message from me and hoped that they would follow through with it when he was awake. That seemed to be the difficulty, catching him when he was actually awake.

David's neighbor and I kept in touch about every other day. She would visit with him, and on occasion, he would be awake. She told him about me, but due to the stroke and his body's condition, he said he no longer remembered me. He had reverted back to his childhood, believing that he still lived at home with his mom, and he wanted to go home. They kept telling him she was gone, but he wouldn't listen. Then he'd fall asleep again.

About a week into this cycle, the neighbor was on her way to visit David again. I asked her if she had a cell phone so I could FaceTime with David. She said yes. I hadn't seen or spoken with him in thirty-two years, so I wasn't sure what to expect, except for a much older version of David who had been put through the wringer of life. When she made it to David's room, he had surprisingly just woken up. She greeted him, and said, "Hi David, I have a surprise for you!" She showed him her phone, and we were instantly FaceTiming! My first impression was that he looked jaundiced, tired, weak, and so much older. I tried not to let my emotions show, so I said, "Hey David! Hi there! Remember me? It's Kari from Peniel!" I was all smiles, and actually a little giddy about it. He looked at me funny like he didn't remember me. So his neighbor said, "Do you remember Kari?" He wasn't able to speak clearly, but mumbled, "No." Well, it had been a long time, but I get told by people I've known for decades that I haven't changed much. I didn't want him to see my disappointment, so I brought up different memories that might trigger a positive response from him. He continued to look at me blankly. I told him that many of his friends from Peniel were praying for him, including me, and with a hoarse voice that was more of a grumble than a word, he said, "Thank you." I kept trying to remind him of people, situations, and events, but none of it seemed to brighten his face with recognition. Nurses were coming and going in the room the whole time we were on the phone, and the noise level was getting pretty high, so David began to get frustrated and started waving his arms at them and frowning even bigger than he had been. At this point, from what I was told later, he believed I was his current girlfriend, that everyone in the room was too loud, and that they needed to quiet down because he couldn't hear his girlfriend! It was truly hard for me to see him like this, and to realize that his mind might never come back. Perhaps with some of the memories he had and some of the things he'd done, this was a good thing, a blessing in disguise.

During the next couple of weeks, David's mind remained the same, although his body made a few improvements. The strength in his legs came back enough to where he would climb out of bed, escape his room, and try to leave the hospital to get home to his mom. The staff had to strap him down for his own safety. He'd find ways to get out of those straps, and then fall out of bed. It was becoming increasingly difficult for them to take care of him, especially when he tried to stab the nurses with his fork for not letting him go home. If he spoke, he was vulgar at times. This did not go over well with those caring for him. There was always blood in his urine, and the many efforts to help his liver heal, failed. I had Face-Timed with him a couple more times, but each day his condition worsened. The doctors just kept telling us his time was very short, and he would never leave the hospital.

Surprise, surprise! When the neighbors went back to visit David, he was gone. The staff indicated that he had been moved to a rehabilitation nursing home because he couldn't continue at the hospital. He had no way of paying any bills, no future, and no memory, but he did have a little life left in him. After his neighbor got in touch with me, I posted an update on Peniel's Facebook page:

"UPDATE ON MY SICK FRIEND: He is still with us. His frame of mind is that of a teenager, so he has no memories of most of his life. He was released from the hospital over a week ago and had been sent to a geriatric rehab center (a type of nursing home) that does minimal care, and even that is extremely lacking. He cannot control his bathroom urges, so he wears a diaper, and the staff didn't seem to change it. His neighbors would visit him nearly every day and find him covered in diarrhea, and his bed very soiled. The staff appears to do nothing for him but supply three meals a day. He has no clothes since his stuff was thrown out of his apartment due to late rent and they all thought he was dying. His legs are getting stronger, so he escapes his room and sneaks into other's rooms, but this makes the residents VERY angry. Needless to say, he has stitches in his mouth and several broken ribs now from getting abused by either his roommate, someone else or a staffer. Unknown who. They sent him back to the hospital two days ago where the doctors say he is badly beaten up and severely dehydrated. His liver is still not well. Now he is strapped down again, with an IV and a catheter. At least he is in a safe place, but with no mobility. He calls one of his nun friends "Kari" and says she is his girlfriend, she loves him and is going to take him away from that place.

I sent him a card, and when he read the portion about the Lord, he said, 'God? He lives in Ohio, and I need a stamp to write him a letter.' Hah! Basically, he is still around for an unknown period of time. Currently, he is set to go back in about two weeks to that same terrible facility because he has no insurance and no one else will take him due to his mental issues at this point. This facility has had multiple reports against it for neglect and abuse. How it is still operating, I don't know. What I do know is that he has nothing. I am putting together a care package for him with the basic supplies he might need since none of that is provided by this geriatric facility, and since he has no shoes, clothes, a decent blanket, books, etc.

This neighboring family is all he has on this planet that is showing any compassion and love toward him. They see him as an uncle to their nine-year-old daughter who just adores him. They would have him over for dinner, he would bring her Barbie gifts, and commented about how he wished he had a daughter of his own. He is this family's closest thing to a family member since both parents have either lost their own or have a bad relationship with them. So, he is their best friend. They have watched him tumble down this dark hole in the last two years, and it has been very difficult for them.

The Lord is still in control of my friend's life. Please pray that his mind be fully restored, that his living conditions improve, that his body be completely healed, and that he would seek out the Lord Jesus again. I am sending him a Bible just in case. He no longer has addictions since he has no memory of them. That is good!"

The staff ignored his cries most of the time. They knew he was troubled and a very difficult patient, so they just left him alone. He would pee on himself, and not get changed. They would put a diaper on him, and his diarrhea would run down his leg, and he'd be wearing the same diaper for hours. The excrement would be dried by the time his neighbor saw him. He didn't brush his teeth, shower, or even wash his hands. The staff just didn't help him with anything, let alone encourage him to help himself.

When his neighbor came to visit him one morning, as I shared in my Facebook post, he was on the floor, curled up in a ball, and she could see severe bruising on his left side, from his hips to nearly his shoulders. She called for help. The staff claimed not to know what happened. They surmised that he had been terribly beaten up by his roommate when he had gotten out of bed and harassed the man. The neighbor went ballistic with the nurses. *Why in the world was he lying on the cold floor?* They realized he had been there for more than a day. The bruising was of great concern, so the doctor sent him back to the hospital. There the doctors learned that he had several broken ribs, his kidneys were failing faster, he was severely dehydrated, and he needed to be sedated and strapped down again for a couple of weeks to recover. *So, why was it that two days later he was back at rehab?* This cycle went on for a couple more weeks, eventually with David remaining in the hospital indefinitely. He fell back into a continual sleep mode with the progression of his failing liver and not eating or drinking. His body then completely shut down. He passed away, alone, on May 3, 2018.

Here is what I shared with the Peniel family:

"David passed away Thursday, May 3rd. He was 54. He is now freed from his addictions! Thank you for your many prayers for David. The Lord's will is done, and David's eternity has begun!!"

Addictions of any kind are harmful to us: drugs and alcohol, sex and porn, our cell phones, Facebook and Twitter, gambling, heck even online games and coffee. These addictions will have a negative effect on your physical, mental, emotional and even spiritual self. None of us are immune to that. David ended up wasting most of his life since he chose to spend it drowning his sorrows. His life-long addictions finally claimed his life, but his battle is over, and now he is with his Lord. That is the hope that we as believers have regardless of our circumstances, regardless of the good or bad choices we make. No one is perfect. Jesus is the reason to keep on fighting, to keep on living, to keep on loving ourselves and those around us. He has given us the opportunity to know Him, to know the Father, and to one day see what we cannot understand now, here, in this life. "*For now, we see in a mirror dimly, but then face to face!*" (1 Corinthians 13:12.)

As I was researching the history of our conversations, I came across a Facebook post from October 2016. I wrote:

"If you woke up this morning knowing it was your last day on earth, What would you do? What would you say?"

David (in his writing) replied:

"I've thought about these kind of questions and believe I've came up with a theory. To love and be loved, to trust and be trusted, to have a feeling of belonging and a sense of purpose and accomplishment."

Perhaps his theory of life is spot on. I do hope that during his life he felt loved, experienced trust, and realized a sense of purpose. Only Heaven knows.

Within three months of David's death, the Lord placed someone else on my path who was struggling, with a history of addictions, bad choices, and about ten other things, that coincidentally or not, we had in common.

a bullfrog and a boy

If you've been around swamps or ponds, you've heard a multitude of varied sounds that fill the air and can even get so loud that they drown out your own thoughts. The toads croaking, the crickets chirping, the birds chattering with their wings flapping, the wind rustling the leaves and swaying the tall grasses, and the splashes and *kerplunks* of water as the turtles and frogs escape to safety from any approaching predators. So, when you hear an unusual sound that doesn't fit the norm, it causes you to pause, and ponder.

This happened to me as I was hiking Sawnee Mountain, which is about 2 miles from our home. This particular trail is on the lesser traveled side of the mountain, so an encounter with anyone is few and far between. I tend to like it this way though because this is my quiet time, my alone time with the Lord. On this day, as I drew near to the hidden pond, I could hear many noises, but the loudest was the sound of a lone bullfrog. That's not unusual, but to hear this sound was. I stopped in my tracks and listened closely. *Crooooak*. Silence. *CROOOOOOAK*. Silence. *CROOOAAAAKKKK*. The cry of this bullfrog made my heart hurt! It was such a painful sound that I had to find it. *What the heck was wrong?* I kept stopping to listen to its cry and closed in on its voice. I was within ten feet of it, but there was so much brush in between us, that I had to get right to the pond's edge and walk a few feet in the muck before I saw the poor thing. When I finally could get a better look at it, I saw that it was nearly completely covered in mud, struggling to climb out of a small muddy hole right near the water's edge. As I stood directly over the bullfrog, I realized the problem—its right back leg was in the mouth of a snake. The frog had been crying out in pain and agony because this predator was trying to drag it into its hole and have it as a meal! I snapped a couple of pictures of it, not believing my eyes, and as soon as I did, the snake saw me, got scared and let go of the frog's leg. The bullfrog immediately hopped away and dove into the safety of the water. The hungry snake quickly retreated into its watery hole in the muck. I marveled at what I had just witnessed and was happy to be of help to this lone bullfrog. Hopefully, it went on to live a much longer and "hoppier" life. Pun intended.

Several months later on a Thursday evening when my husband had to work late, I decided to take the kids out for dinner, and they chose Wendy's. When we arrived, there weren't too many people there, and thankfully no line. Karli quietly pointed out to me a handsome young man sitting by himself at a table, with his sandy blonde hair in a man-bun. I acknowledged seeing him, and then we ordered our food. As we passed by his table to sit down, I looked at him and smiled. He looked so sad and alone! After we sat down, I got up to get some ketchup, and when I glanced at him again, I realized he was crying. His eyes were all red, and tears were slowly going down his cheek.

He didn't say anything, but just sat there, deeply saddened by something. Now I know most guys don't cry, especially in public, so I knew he was in a bad way. I put the ketchup on our table and went back to this young man. As I leaned over the table to talk to him, his blue eyes met mine. I asked him if he was OK, and he said, "No." I wasn't expecting that honest answer, so I asked what was wrong and if there was something I could do for him, and he again said, "No." I didn't believe him. He didn't have any food or drink at the table, so I asked him if I could buy an ice cream or something for him, but just decided to get him a meal and a drink anyway. When his food was ready, I took it to him, and he seemed grateful, although he was slow to eat it. We spoke a little bit more, and I prayed with him, then went back to my table with the kids. They were naturally filled with many questions about what I was doing, who was he, what were we talking about, etc. I told them what little I knew, and said I needed to go back and talk to him some more.

He decided to open up a little bit, telling me how he arrived in the nearby town of Gainesville a couple of days ago, of his walking all day to get here from the Gainesville bus station ten miles away, of him not getting his old job back at the grocery store, and how he was sleeping behind the Wendy's dumpster on a pallet. *What??? This kid is homeless?* He told me he had been kicked out of his home at seventeen, and that he was nineteen now. He'd been homeless off and on for about two years, and had held some jobs, but due to drugs, drinking and his temper, he lost them. He said he was considering suicide again. I definitely was not expecting such openness from this young man! It reminded me of that evil snake with the bullfrog, and how the evil one now had a stronghold on this boy's heart! It was trying to pull him under, to finish him off. This was really bad. Knowing this young man was deeply hurting, I could not just walk away from him!! I told him to eat and that I would be back in a few minutes. I sat with the kids, told them his story, wolfed down my meal, and called my husband.

Any really good, caring, responsible man/husband/father would naturally be hesitant to consider what I was proposing to mine. I calmly told him about this boy, and as I was telling him his story, my daughter chimed in, telling Drew that we needed to help him. We needed to bring him home with us. He could NOT stay there, contemplating suicide and possibly dying without us at least trying to help him! His front tooth had been badly chipped and he was dirty. He was alone, homeless, and hopeless. He had no money, no apparent friends, and saw no future. As Karli and I tried to convince Drew that this boy needed us, Drew decided to meet us at Wendy's on his way home and perhaps talk some sense into us. He was adamant that this was not a good idea nor a safe one. I agreed with him 100%. It was not a good idea, but one that I felt compelled to act on.

While I was sitting there eating, my mind was whirling around, not with the "what ifs," but rather the "hows" to make it work, and the "whys" if we chose not to help. The best thing I could do at that moment was to pray about it . . . pray earnestly and intently, with unwavering faith. If this was going to really happen, then the Lord would have to soften Drew's heart, because without his approval, this wouldn't ever happen. I asked the kids their opinion on the situation and what they thought about us inviting him to our house, at least for the night. They were both OK with it. So, after the kids and I finished eating, the three of us went over to this young man's table and sat down with him. I introduced them to him, and he said his name was Keith. We sat together, in Wendy's, trying to make friends with a total stranger, who was badly in need of some help.

My husband arrived quickly, much to my surprise, and joined us at Keith's table. This was really the best scenario, for Drew to meet and talk with Keith, to see what the kids and I saw and why we felt the need to help out this young man. I could sense Drew's heart softening as they spoke. Then, we looked at each other, and I knew that he was ready to open our home, if even for just one night, to this kid in need. We asked him if he wanted to come to our house and shower, get some sleep, and prepare himself to face another day. He agreed, with the biggest grin I had ever seen! He went behind the dumpster and got his small backpack of belongings and climbed into Drew's car.

When we got home, I quickly cleaned up the shared bathroom between the Jack and Jill rooms. Dane slept in one, and the other room that had two twin beds in it would be Keith's room. I got him some clean towels, and we let him get settled in. Drew went downstairs to exercise, so Karli and I went down there with him to talk about our spur-of-the-moment decision. As we were sharing, I remembered something that instantly gave me goosebumps. I stood there with my mouth wide open, in shock. Drew and Karli looked at me funny. That morning, I explained, Dane and I had our devotions, which consisted of brief prayer time and reading some Bible passages. Usually, we would read a chapter from Psalms, one from

Proverbs, and a chapter from one of the gospels. What I had realized was that our scripture that morning was the story of the Good Samaritan. Now, Dane was witnessing us living out that parable and seeing just who our "neighbor" is!

Over the next couple of days, Keith met many new people who would be a positive influence in his life. First, we called a neighbor who regularly works with the homeless in downtown Atlanta and has such a passion for them. She came over the first night to get an idea of where he was at mentally and emotionally, to see if he needed to be hospitalized, have therapy, get on some medication, or just figure out more details of his life. Then he met with a dear friend of mine who is also a certified counselor. Both women were very concerned for his well-being and agreed that he needed much more than our little family could give him. We knew that but we just couldn't send him to a psychiatric situation that might potentially make his state of mind worse. We believed he needed some real love, a family setting, and some time to heal and recover, then get back on his feet.

Two days after coming to our home, he met with a lady who works at Mountain Education Charter High School, an online institution with a local school setting where he could get his diploma. Keith had zero interest in getting his GED, because he knew that it was time-consuming and would limit his future endeavors. He also knew his actual high school diploma could open up more doors and allow him to go to a trade school. Our first goal was to get him enrolled. It didn't take long for the school to get his documents sent from South Carolina, so within one week of being with us, he was ready to return to high school for the next two years. Every step we took for him meant that he was plugging into our area, our city, our church, our friends, and this would make it difficult for him to go somewhere else. But, we knew that these steps were necessary to get him moving forward into a better future for himself, whether he stayed with us longer or for just a few days.

Some of Keith's story that he shared with us dealt with drug addictions and alcoholism as a teenager. We were obviously concerned that these past bad habits might raise their ugly heads again while in our house, so we set up a few rules for Keith, but also researched and inquired about him going to either a transitional living home for men or a drug and alcohol rehab for men. There were many potential places for him to go, but after we would research each one and call them or learn more about them, their feedback was, "He's not addicted now so we can't take him," or "You have to pay a deposit to have him stay," or "No, he's not the right fit." The more I prayed about the Lord finding him the right place to stay, the more I realized that He already did. It was with us, for a time. We had the room in our huge house, I had the time to shuttle him everywhere since I didn't work, and we had the resources and friends who could help fill in the blanks. We just needed to find it in our hearts to accept him as a member of our family, as he had already accepted us as his temporary family. He was now calling me his temporary mom, and the kids he called his brother and sister. With no other options known, we realized this could mean he was staying with us for a long while, possibly up to six months.

The more I heard Keith's history, the more I recognized that he and I had so many similarities in our stories:

1. We were both unwanted, unplanned pregnancies.
2. We both lived in unhealthy living environments.
3. We both lived in foster care.
4. We both were adopted.
5. We both were molested by an adopted family member.
6. We both either considered or attempted suicide by hanging.
7. We both were given up by adopted family.
8. We both had very harmful habits.
9. We both had a badly chipped front tooth (mine had been repaired long ago).
10. We both were sought after by the Lord.
11. We both were taken in by loving anonymous families.

Keith attended Mountain Lake Church his first Sunday with us. The message that day that could have been written just for him. Keith commented that maybe he needed to accept Jesus. *WOW! That was fast!* The Lord was really working in his heart. So the following Sunday, Keith met with the Student Pastor at our church, prayed to accept Jesus as his Lord and Savior, and showed it by publicly getting baptized thirty minutes later in front of about 200 people! He came up out of that water, and raised his fist high and said, "YEAH!!" What a beautiful moment! I admit to crying just a bit and laughing at the same time. Just one and a half weeks prior, he had been contemplating suicide, and now he was celebrating his new life! Just like that wily snake that had a grip on the bullfrog's leg had let him go, the evil one no longer had a stranglehold on Keith's life. He has been freed to live!

That list of our lives' similarities made me realize that the events in my past can still be used to help others as long as I am willing to be used. *How many other people, who saw Keith that day as he sat in Wendy's for eight hours, just passed him by and didn't give him another thought?* I am not tooting my own horn but I am saying that one who has been through so many difficult challenges in life can recognize when someone else is in need of help and can be empathetic to his or her situation. When our stories can directly help people during their darkest moments, that is the ultimate gift that we can give to them. Compassion. Empathy. Love.

Our church family had really taken to Keith. Through the CARE ministry, we found a local dentist who was willing to repair his chipped front tooth, fill a cavity, and provide him with a cleaning. You should see his smile now! It's amazing what a little love can do for someone's self-esteem. Also, several men took him under their wings and worked with him, prayed for him, and encouraged him to tell his story to teens who might need to hear it. In doing so it might prevent teens from making some of the same mistakes he had, or to remind them that they are not alone in their pain and struggles, and others have been where they are and have come out on the other side, with the help of the Lord and a few strangers He might put in their lives.

The Place of Forsyth County, a non-profit Social Service Organization, has served residents of our county since 1975. It provides assistance to families with basic emergency needs in difficult times. It offers them work-readiness training and job placement services. It also operates a food pantry and a thrift store and makes counseling available to those who need it. This group was made aware of Keith's situation nearly a year before we met him, and at that time, had provided him with a tent he used to sleep in for nearly two months, a bike for transportation, and some basic necessities. Now, many months later, I was advised to turn to them for help. Two different friends of mine with close ties to the organization encouraged me to reach out to its manager, so I called her, Joni Smith, and set up a meeting with her. Since Keith was OK with seeing them again, our hopes were high that somehow they could help him once again.

They did more than help him. They offered him a part-time job! His hourly wage was $9 per hour, but for someone who didn't have much or need much, that was enough to get him started. He worked the 10 am to 2 pm shift four days a week, which allowed him the time to go to school in the evenings from 4:30 pm to 9:00 pm. It was the perfect scenario for Keith.

This schedule also meant that he could sleep in a little later in the mornings, including the days he worked. Nice for him, but my issue with this was I had to wake him up every morning, literally every morning, continually, with multiple attempts each time to get him up for work. Since he couldn't drive, I had to drive him everywhere. I didn't mind doing this as I knew this was part of helping him, but I did mind having to keep waking him up every day. I figured that by the time you are nineteen, you should be past the age of needing "mom" to get you up. After a few weeks of this, it started to wear me down and was making Drew angry. Keith's problem wasn't just getting up but going to sleep. We looked at possible reasons for his insomnia and encouraged him to make healthy eating choices and stay off the electronics, including the television, Xbox, and his portable Play Station.

Another big issue for me was getting Keith to drive. He was totally dependent on someone getting him to work, picking him up, taking him to school, picking him back up, and taking him to any appointments and church. This fell to me since I was the one at home during the day. I knew this would be a part of it in the beginning but I had to get busy real fast to help him start driving. The number one problem was that he had lost his birth certificate, therefore couldn't get a permit let alone a driver's license. We began the process of filling out the necessary paperwork to get a replacement one from his home state of North Carolina. Meanwhile, he needed to practice driving. Drew was not excited about this prospect, since it meant my 2015 Toyota Highlander Limited Edition would be his demolition derby car to gain driving experience. *Oh boy* . . . Hesitantly, I drove him to a large local church parking lot, let him get in the driver's seat, and off we went. Slowly. VERY slowly.

Even with some driving time behind the wheel, Keith would need his own set of wheels. Knowing he had absolutely no money and no way of earning enough in a few weeks or even a few months, Drew set up a GoFundMe account for him, explaining Keith's story and our desire for him to get a dependable car. Within three days, we raised $1,770 of the $5,000 goal. Then, the money just stopped. *This was puzzling.* We decided to wait it out since he didn't have a replacement birth certificate yet anyway.

About four weeks into our journey with Keith, he was with the high school kids at church when he began feeling dizzy during worship. He fell backwards on the floor and had a full-on seizure for more than two minutes! When he came to, he remembered feeling faint and seeing the strobe lights, but remembered nothing else during the seizure. The worst part was he had very little sensation in his legs and couldn't walk. The staff called 911 and then Drew. The four of us quickly rushed over there in time to see Keith getting placed in the ambulance. His eyes were very red, most likely from crying due to the trauma of it all, and he seemed pretty out of it. We followed the ambulance to the ER.

We waited as the doctor and nurses did their immediate assessment. Within a few minutes, the staff allowed us into his room where they had been running tests and giving him fluids through an IV. We explained to them who we were, that he was staying with us, and currently were his caretakers. As they continued to ask him questions about his history, he admitted to having three to four seizures in one week a few months ago when he lived in southern Georgia. This was news to us. He stated he did go to the ER after most of those episodes, but they didn't diagnose the cause. He needed to see a neurologist for that. The doctor was concerned about Keith's legs because he said they were numb-like. Keith had very little sensation in them and he couldn't move them without great effort. Within an hour, some of the motor skills with his legs returned, but not without a sharp pain in his right thigh and hip, and only partial movement in his left leg. By now, his headache had begun too. As I researched seizures, it appeared that all of his symptoms were common side effects that could last for days, up to weeks. This could be a long recovery and probably delay him from getting on his feet and becoming independent any time soon.

As we sat with Keith in the ER, he reminded me that his girl-friend had gone to the ER earlier that afternoon. She was a gal he met at school a couple of weeks earlier, and she had her enlarged tonsils removed a few days prior. Her throat kept swelling so badly that she couldn't breathe, and this time it was after a nap, so her worried mother took her to the hospital. Keith and I began to talk about that, and wondered what other hospital she would have gone to. There really wasn't an ER any closer, so maybe she had come to this one. I went out into the hallway, and there to my left stood the girl's mom! They were in the room next to Keith's! OK. I know you're think-ing that this wasn't a coincidence–perhaps he faked the whole thing just to see her? The thought did cross my mind, multiple times, but as the doctors did their exam, they concluded that this was the real thing. The girlfriend's mom and I spoke for a few minutes, when along came her daughter, looking like she was relieved to be able to breathe better. She genuinely seemed curious why we were there and thought it was to see her! We explained what had happened, and we chuckled at the irony of it all, but wished neither one of them had to be there under those circumstances. That's the last we saw of them that night. She checked out before Keith did. We left about thirty minutes later, with Keith walking out of the ER on his own but with a limp, a pending large hospital bill (not for us!) and no helpful information as to why this happened. The CT scan came back normal as did the blood work. Some-how, we had to get him to see a neurologist.

The next morning, we let Keith sleep in. No work today. After a night like he had, he needed rest and time to allow his body to recover. Around 10:30 am, I checked on him. The blinds were closed, but when Keith opened his eyes, he immediately complained about how bright it was, and he had a terrible headache. Migraines are a common post-seizure side effect, as is sensitivity to light. It took a couple of days for that sensitivity to calm down, and his headaches to go away.

Joni, Executive Director of The Place, and the counselor decided that now Keith needed a physical to see what else might be going on with his body, and to be sure that it was OK for him to come back to work. It had been a few years since he had a physical. We were hoping the doctors could refer him to a neurologist, and that just maybe the hospital would cover the expense due to his current homeless status. For now, he had been using our address, but this was temporary. A regular doctor's appointment was set up, we went, but when we were done, everything had come back normal. *OK, that's something positive.* What they also did was give him a referral, and a form to fill out for financial assistance to see a neurologist. *Yay!!* Perhaps he would finally be able to get to the root cause of his seizures. Maybe it would be normal, and we could move forward with his driver's license! Perhaps not, and he might never be able to drive. It was a risk finding out, but necessary.

Another part of Keith's story has to do with his mental health, his state of mind. Because of his troubling past, the sexual abuse, the drug addictions, the drinking binges, being taken from his birth mom, living with a foster family, getting adopted, struggling in school, his buddy dying, leaving home at seventeen, being homeless off and on, and getting beat up, he really needed to talk to someone. I shared my story with Keith and tried to counsel him from a "mom's" point of view, but what he really needed was a professional. He admitted to seeing counselors before when he was younger but didn't believe that they really cared about him, therefore, he didn't care to talk to them. They all wanted to put him away somewhere. That counselor friend of mine who met him the day after we brought him home agreed to see him for next to nothing out of concern for his well-being and ours too I suspect. What he really needed was a psychiatrist. But, like most people who don't want to face their past or deal with it and just push it under the rug, Keith's sessions quickly ended—actually, the week of his seizure. It was apparent to my friend that he wasn't willing to do the hard work to get better. He began to have these dark thoughts again, of hurting himself, and he refused to consider any medications. By now, Drew and I were getting more concerned. Keith had a history of violence but had never shown any of that toward us. I didn't think he would hurt us, but heck, we'd only known him for a little over a month. *Was he schizophrenic?*

I received a text from my next door neighbor at 7:20 am on our 26th wedding anniversary that read, "Is everything OK this morning? Noticed the sheets hanging out the upstairs window . . ." I had been up for a few minutes and was about to say good morning to Karli, when I suddenly ran out the back door and looked up to Keith's room, seeing nothing unusual. I went around to the front of the house thinking maybe she meant Dane's windows and saw nothing. I caught a glimpse of something on the side of the house. Walking through the dewy wet grass, I kept my eyes focused on whatever that was. There, hanging out of the second-floor bathroom window, was a rope made of sheets and blankets that stretched down to our air conditioning units. I noticed the screen resting on the bushes and a boxcutter on the ground. Keith had snuck out during the night and taken off! A flood of emotions ran through me, from shock to sorrow to guilt, remembering our conversation from the night before.

Up to this point, my role as "mom" was pretty literal, from waking him up every day for work, to making sure he showered occasionally. Our purpose of bringing him home was to help get him back on his feet as an independent, responsible young man. As the weeks had gone by, I began feeling frustrated with the basic task of having to wake him up. This kid could sleep through anything! It didn't help that he went to bed so late and claimed to have sleep insomnia. Now being a menopausal woman, I can certainly relate to sleep problems. But, staying up all hours of the night, then not getting up in the morning at a reasonable time for a job that didn't start until 10:00 am—let alone prepare your own lunch for that day—made me question his ability to be on his own. So I had prepared a list of goals and skills that most teenagers would need to have accomplished to be ready for their independence. Mind you I altered this list for his needs. Drew, Keith and I sat down one Saturday, and we talked about these goals and how important they were for any young person to attain to a degree by the time they were eighteen. Our immediate number one goal was for him to wake himself up for work, church or any appointment he might have. OK. Even my thirteen-year-old son can get himself up for school by 7:30 in the morning. But, he had been taught to maintain this schedule, and his body was prepared for it. Keith hadn't had this routine in months, so I knew it would take time, but by five weeks, you'd think he would be taking it more seriously.

After several more mornings of him not getting up, Drew and I sat him down again, on the eve of our anniversary, and said,

"How's it going with your goals? What are you working on? We've noticed you still aren't waking up on your own . . . What can you do to make yourself get up? Set three alarms for the time?" It was at this point that Drew said to me, "Kari, tomorrow just don't wake him up. He has to do this. If he is late for work or misses it altogether, then he will have to pay those consequences, maybe even he'll lose his job if it continues to happen." We were trying to show him the critical need to get this first very important step in life down: **Wake up. Get moving. Find a reason to crawl out of bed! "Mom" won't be there forever to do these things for you.** Keith had very little to say during this meeting. He hung his head down low. He decided there was no other choice but to leave.

These memories and raw emotions now filled my entire being while staring up at that homemade rope hanging out of our window. *At least Keith hadn't hung himself!* I quickly went back in the house to surmise just what had happened. Karli was just coming out of her bedroom, so without telling her why I told her to follow me. We tried his door, but it was locked. Dane's door was open, so we went into the Jack-and-Jill bathroom that way. At this point, Karli didn't know what was going on. We walked into the bathroom, saw the toilet/tub door closed with the light on, and opened it. Keith had made a rope out of sheets and a blanket, tied it to the toilet tank, and had opened Dane's tiny bathroom window. Karli gasped (she thought he had hung himself), looked out the window expecting to see him there, and was relieved not to see him. Instead, she saw the homemade rope that hung down the outside wall. Keith had thrown his backpack filled with most of his things out the window, climbed down onto the air conditioning units, and walked away during the night. The box cutter I found apparently fell out of his backpack. Good thing! He had a history of intentionally hurting himself with sharp objects by slicing his forearms.

The morning was busy informing the many people that had been helping him of his latest poor decision. I emailed, called or texted The Place, his school, the doctors, his counselor, my neighbors, our church, etc. Then I texted Keith, doubting that I would ever hear from him again. I wanted to be sure he was OK and wondered if he was going to go back to work as well as keep up with school. I was also pretty angry that he left us like that, and after so much time and emotion that we had invested in him, I was hurt. To my surprise, he soon responded back with an apology and said he felt he had to leave because of what my husband had said, about me not waking him up the next day. He felt there was no way he could manage that. We texted for a few minutes about the situation, but by the time we were done, I felt this huge weight fall off of my shoulders. He was safe. He was ok. For this, my heart was glad. Although it took me a couple of weeks to process this change and not cry every time his name came up, the Lord had shown me the need to accept Keith's decision to leave. I had to let him go. I could no longer worry about him. My time was done. He was nineteen, an adult, and even though I don't agree with why he left or what his plans were, I trusted that the Lord allowed his departure from our home both for our benefit as well as for Keith's future. Within a few weeks, we learned he had gone to downtown Atlanta and was once again homeless, and all of his belongings, including his new phone and Bible, had been stolen.

We decided it would be best since he left of his own accord without our blessing, and since his future of driving was now still in question, that the GoFundMe money needed to be returned to those who donated it. With a note explaining our decision, it was all returned. The thought crossed my mind about why the money had stopped coming in after just a few days, and then I understood.

Keith works hard when he wants to, has dreams of bigger things, and says he wants a family of his own. If he will listen to that still small voice of the Lord and seek Him and continue to read God's manual for living, then he just might achieve those goals and dreams. God's not done with him! He answered our prayer of helping Keith get to that next point, his next chapter. For us, except for continued prayer for him, that chapter of our life is done. He will always be a part of our family, our story, and he will remain in my heart and is and will be indefinitely in my prayers.

The Lord most definitely pursued Keith and I believe He will continue to do so. To witness this, and to be a small part of it, is a true gift. My job was just to be obedient and to love unconditionally. God was actually the one doing all the work! He arranged for his schooling, his counseling, his lodging, his mentors, and his job. He had Keith's seizure occur in a safe place when others were around and would get him help.

Any time I hear the song, *"Reckless Love"* by Cory Asbury, I think of and pray for Keith. This had become his favorite song. He is a child of God, whether he is living with us, or homeless by choice.

I hope the evil one, like that hungry snake, won't find him back in the mud and drag him under.

My prayer is that the Lord will watch over him and continue to be that Father Keith so desperately needs.

reflecting on the journey

The number one question that I get asked after people hear even a portion of my story is, "How come you seem so normal after having been through so much?" *Believe* me when I say I wouldn't be here today if Jesus didn't take my hand, carry me through the muddy waters, lead me down the winding roads, and guide me through the storms. He provided hundreds of people along the way who taught me, encouraged me, hugged me, sheltered me, loved me, provided for me, donated to me, wept with me and especially prayed for me. I had so many women who took me under their wings and loved me as a daughter! My birth mother Ruth giving me up, my first adopted family having me for a short time, mom and dad adopting me, Mrs. Melodee teaching me at Peniel, Hazel and four other women taking me into their homes to live, my birth mother's and birth father's families loving me, my mother-in-law Janet accepting me into her family, and the Lord regarding me as His child, all attest that I am a daughter to many!

Consider this: I was not aborted! That, in and of itself, is a great beginning. I was granted life, the unexpected result of a one-night stand. Consider the rest: I was adopted two different times within two years. I was sent to a boarding school, removing me from a sexually abusive relationship. I met Jesus at thirteen years old, and He protected me in spite of my foolishness when I ran away from boarding school. I was able to forgive my father for molesting me. The Lord provided for me in every way in Kansas City through strangers and friends who offered me food, shelter, money, and transportation. He gave me the man I needed and wanted. We found all of my birth families! I was introduced to my birth mother's family at a reunion, not three hours from where I lived. I was introduced to my birth father and his family just three months later in the same city we had planned to vacation in, near my mom and brother. My daughter was able to meet both of her great-grandmothers just before they died during the same Christmas season. The Lord provided a job for my husband in the Atlanta area that led us to a new church family we became deeply rooted in. He taught me that a church family is important, but that being willing to go where He leads you is more important. The Lord reconnected me with an old friend who needed to be reminded of who he was in Christ before he died. He brought a young man into our lives who needed someone who could understand his past and be not only compassionate but empathetic and hopeful. My history and experiences were invaluable in connecting with Keith. That verifies there were many purposes for my life's difficulties.

It was during our time with young Keith that the desire to finish my story hit me once again. Perhaps the events of the last two years needed to happen for this story to be told in full. Only the Lord knows, and perhaps you as the reader.

Lastly, my story is being shared with you because God has chosen for it to be told so that He would be glorified by it. He worked on the hearts of many to help encourage the writing of this book, to help proofread it so that only the truth be told, and to allow it to be shared in spite of any reflection it may have on an individual. This is not *my* story, but rather *His* story of how He has worked in my life.

God's plan, His way of weaving my adoptions and often difficult, bizarre circumstances into such an amazing story, has allowed me to tell so many people of His love, mercy, grace, and forgiveness. He has used this to encourage other women and children who have had similar circumstances with a family member or friend, or who still need to learn to forgive. What a gift! What an honor for me to be able to help even one! He has used this story to lead other adopted people to try and find their birth families, regardless of the potential outcome. He has used this story to convict those who turn their faces or shut their hearts' doors to others in need. Thank you, Lord God, for being in control of my life. Thank you for adopting me into your family! Thank you for providing those who regard me as their own. Thank you for having a plan for even me.

His ways are not *our* ways. Sure, I would not have asked for my past, but He let me go through it. Without the past, there couldn't be a future. Without the intense pain, there couldn't be deep healing. Without the sadness, there couldn't be great joy! Without the loss, there couldn't be something better to be discovered! We must trust that there is something far greater to gain, and that comes only through believing that we do have a hope in knowing, loving and following our Lord and Savior, Jesus Christ.

"Trust in the Lord with all your heart and lean not on your own understanding. In all your ways acknowledge Him, and He will make your paths straight." (Proverbs 3:5-6 NAS)

I do not believe in coincidences. I do believe that our God is in control of all things. He sees the bigger picture and includes each of us in His grand story of redemption if we are only willing to trust Him. Even though we may not understand what is going on or why, the Lord does. One day all of these puzzle pieces will fit together to reveal the most magnificent picture.

"And we know that for those who love God, all things work together for good, for those who are called according to his purpose." (Romans 8:28 ESV)

As Grandpa William, who is now 97, puts it: "How can we mind the journey when the path leads us home?"

"Then the trees of the forest will sing for joy before the Lord: For He is coming to judge the earth. O give thanks to the Lord, for He is good; For His loving-kindness is everlasting." (1 Chronicles 16:33-34 NAS)

AUTHOR BIO

Kari Wiseman was born in South Dakota and slowly migrated south to Atlanta, Georgia. She is a stay-at-home mom with her husband of 26 years and their 2 children. You can usually find her hiking, playing games with her kids, and carrying her camera around while searching for unusual moments or angles that catch her eye.

Kari's unique perspective due to a complicated personal life has inspired many. She worked in the television industry for eleven years, was a granite sales consultant for homes and businesses, and was a Nurse Aide in a nursing home.

Kari has had the privilege of sharing her story of adoption, finding family, abuse, and forgiveness with thousands of people. She also has a daily blog that integrates words of inspiration with her passion of photography.

To follow Kari's blog, go to:

SNAPINSPIRE.COM

Daily snapshots of life complemented with inspirational tips for better living.

TIMELINE

KIMBERLY SUE DAVIS
- 04/10/66 born @ 6 lbs, 3 oz, and 19" long in Sioux Falls, S.D.
- 04/15/66 surrendered to Lutheran Social Services by Ruth Davis, mother
- 04/15/66 taken to Henry Kapsch Boarding Home

ANDREA JUNE MATSON
- 04/27/66 placed in Matson's home in Rapid City, S.D. and name changed to Andrea June
- 01/18/67 adopted by the Matson family
- 01/14/68 returned to Lutheran Social Services
- 01/14/68 placed in Rogers' home, foster family
- 02/21/68 first visited by the Larsen family
- 02/25/68 officially surrendered by the Matsons

KARI ELLEN LARSEN
- 02/26/68 placed in Larsen's home in Sioux Falls, S.D. and name changed to Kari Ellen
- 10/02/68 adopted by the Larsen family
- 1969 moved to White Bear Lake, MN, into an apartment
- 1971 moved into new house in White Bear Lake, MN.
- 05/21/79 sent to Peniel Christian School in Spring Valley, WI.

- 09/24/79 adopted into the Lord's family when I accepted Him as my Savior
- Fall 1982 moved home to White Bear Lake, MN. for three months due to Peniel closing
- Fall 1982 moved back to Peniel when it reopened three months later
- June 1983 moved to Peniel's 2nd location in Onarga, IL.
- 02/13/84 changed school to Hillcrest Lutheran Academy in Fergus Falls, MN.
- 05/27/84 graduated from high school at Hillcrest Lutheran Academy, Fergus Falls, MN.
- June 1985 moved back to Peniel in Spring Valley, WI, to be a girls' counselor
- June 1986 moved to Kansas City, KS, to work with youth, attended C.U.B.I., worked at KYFC-TV 50
- March 1990 moved to Nashville, TN.

KARI ELLEN WISEMAN
- 08/29/92 got married to Drew Wiseman, last name changed
- 06/15/96 met birth mother's family at a reunion in Pigeon Forge, TN.
- 09/20/96 met birth father and family in Bloomington, MN.
- 09/19/01 daughter Karli Belle born
- 05/12/05 son Dane Jennings born
- 05/12/06 moved to Marietta, GA.
- 10/31/10 baptized publicly
- July 2016 moved to Cumming, GA.
- July 2018 met Keith

9 781950 385065